THE SUCCESSFUL
MANAGER

Practical Approaches for Building

and Leading High-Performing Teams

JAMES POTTER AND **MIKE KAVANAGH**

The Successful Manager
Practical Approaches for Building and Leading
High-Performing Teams
Paperback Edition

Copyright © 2020 by Potter Consulting LLC

ISBN: 9798557682312

To my family, mentors, and team members who have enabled, advised, and supported me through my journey as a manager and leader.

TABLE OF CONTENTS

Foreword

Many years ago, at the end of my performance review, my boss shared some news with me.

"We're promoting you," he said, handing me a letter with my new salary and title. A wave of excitement washed over me. This was the moment I had been working so hard for over the previous couple of years.

"Along with this promotion," he continued, "you're going to be taking on a few direct reports effective immediately. I'll be communicating this news to them later today."

In an instant, my excitement gave way to anxiety. I had never managed anyone before.

Then my boss listed the names of the people who would be on my team. Two of them were peers of mine whom I had worked alongside for the past twelve months.

The anxiety now gave way to fear.

"Is there any kind of training I'll receive or any good books you recommend on managing people?" I asked.

"No not really, but don't worry. You'll figure it out as you go," he said as he sent me on my way.

Like new parents being sent home from the hospital with their first child, I had just been thrust into one of the most significant transitions people can go through in their professional lives with little clue what I was doing and virtually no resources to help me navigate the territory.

In the many years since that day, I have worked for a number of organizations and have promoted dozens of people into their first role as a manager. Unfortunately, their transitions were similar to mine.

I have also consulted for over one hundred companies of all sizes and I have found that this approach to manager promotions is the norm. Few organizations provide new managers with the resources to help ensure their success during this period of massive change. New managers are left to "figure it out" in the wild.

This makes for a slow learning curve and a bumpy ride for new managers and for the people who report to them. Most of the time, managers do not know what they are doing well and what they need to improve upon because there isn't a natural way for them to be provided with useful feedback. It isn't common for direct reports to share open and honest feedback with their managers for obvious reasons. And while a 360 review process can create an anonymous opportunity for gathering this feedback, good 360 processes are an anomaly. Not only that, but they tend not to reach far enough down in organizations to apply to new managers because of the time and expense associated with administering them.

This aim of this book is to fill that gap. Rather than being left to figure things out on your own, this book provides you with clear, practical and accessible advice on how to build and lead successful teams. It is the book I wish that I'd had when I first became a manager, as well as the book I wish I could have relied on for guidance during many stages of my journey to becoming a senior leader in large organizations.

Whether you are just starting out as a manager or you're looking to elevate your capabilities and become a top-tier leader of teams, it is my sincere hope that this book helps you reach your goals.

Here are a few things you can expect to take away from this book:

- A clear framework to guide you in building the fundamental competencies of an outstanding manager.
- Practical examples, stories, and tips from some of the world's greatest managers of teams and large organizations.
- Diagnostics to foster self-reflection and to gauge your progress on your journey to becoming a top-tier manager.
- Descriptions of the challenges you can expect to experience as a manager and advice on how to adopt the mindset that will help you triumph and emerge as a truly great manager.

If you are a new manager or you are an MBA student expecting to make this transition soon, your path doesn't have to be a painful ride up the learning curve. Armed with the tools explained in this book, management can be a rewarding journey and one of the biggest opportunities for personal growth available to you in your professional life. All you need in order to get the most out of this book is the willingness to think deeply and critically about the type of manager you want to be and the commitment to follow through with the techniques that will support you in reaching your goal.

Likewise, if you already have plenty of management experience and are simply looking to take your skills to the next level, the same tools and mindset apply. Just as becoming an expert in martial arts hinges most upon having a set of foundational skills and principles drilled in over time, it's mastery of the fundamentals that sets the great managers apart from the rest of the pack.

The world's best leaders have made it a lifelong practice to get better, inspire people, and win as a team. Regardless of where you are on your management journey, we are excited to see what you can achieve when you follow in their footsteps, embrace this mindset, and employ the tools and approaches contained in this book.

Chapter 1:

Why Become a Top-Tier Manager

"Management is the most noble of professions if it's practiced well. No other occupation offers as many ways to help others learn and grow, take responsibility and be recognized for achievement, and contribute to the success of a team."
–Clayton Christensen in How Will You Measure Your Life? (Harvard Business Review, 2010)

So you're a manager or you're about to become one? If that's the case, I'm here to tell you that **becoming a top-tier manager should be your number one professional goal.** Every other priority pales in comparison.

Does that sound like a bold claim? Perhaps. Why do I declare it with such confidence?

Because by definition, your skills in guiding other people will be the single biggest driver of your success from this point forward.

Earlier in your professional life when you were an individual contributor, your performance was driven entirely by you. For the most part, you controlled your destiny: If you worked hard and applied your unique talents and skills to doing a stellar job, your results reflected this, and chances are you were rewarded for your efforts (provided you worked for a decent boss).

But as a manager, your success now depends upon the results of others. If the team succeeds, you succeed. And that is precisely your role as a manager—to build and grow an outstanding team and to elicit the best team performance possible to achieve the desired results. If you have the skills of a top-tier manager, you will maximize the success of the team you are leading. If you don't, your team will not perform, and your individual success will be hampered. It doesn't matter if you're managing a single person or a huge organization; the same principle applies. Become a great manager and you will set yourself up for sustained success over time.

"But I don't just want to be a great manager, I want to be a great *leader*," I hear some of you say.

As the science of management and leadership has evolved over the past several decades, many people have drawn this distinction. Those people tend to imply that managers are simply people who have other people reporting to them, or that managers default to using authority or control to get people to do what they want, whereas leaders drive results through inspiring, motivating, and influencing their teams and the wider organization.

But a manager who relies only on authority or control to get their team to do what they want is a bad manager, and bad management capability makes for a weak leader. Becoming a truly great manager builds the foundation for being a great leader. If you focus on adopting and applying the skills in this book, you'll be well on your way to becoming an outstanding manager and leader, at which point we'll happily call you whatever you want because we all might be working for you.

If you are new to management, it's important to recognize how crucial it is to take this goal of becoming a top-tier manager to heart and build the skills of a great manager as early as possible on your journey. There are two primary reasons for this.

The first reason is that learning to master management skills is like learning to master a language.

Most of us grow up learning a primary language in our household. Later, we may learn additional languages, but beyond a certain point in our lives this tends to require a much greater level of effort. Our brains become wired a certain way and they are harder to retrain. And even if we do become proficient in another language, we may never shake the accent we have as a non-native speaker and we will always feel more comfortable expressing and understanding things using our native language.

It is similar with developing strong managerial skills and habits. The longer you wait to develop optimal skills and habits, the more engrained the sub-optimal habits will become, and the harder it will be to retrain yourself. Beyond a certain point, it can feel as difficult to change those habits as it would be to become fluent in a new language.

Also, much the way knowing how to speak a language only becomes relevant in conversation, management is a two-way communication between you and the individuals on your team. Your teammates need to understand and become fluent in the language as well for productive dialog to occur. If you begin operating with certain behaviors and tactics, your team will become accustomed to that approach, and over time it becomes harder for them to adapt to a new style. They will have developed habits and a comfort zone just like you have.

The second reason to focus on becoming a top-tier manager as early in your career as possible is that you only have a short window before you can become pigeonholed as a bad manager, and it can be difficult to break free from that box. Have you ever seen the fifty-year-old manager who is intelligent and has a ton of expertise and tacit knowledge, but has been bounced around the organization like a utility infielder without being given roles of increasing responsibility? What's holding that person back?

It's easy to blame a lack of ambition, but low ambition is commonly the result of a plateau in career growth rather than the cause of it. Sometimes a person is simply held back because of an abrasive personality or an inability to mesh with other people. But very often it is because they are not seen as having the strong management skills necessary to take on broader leadership roles.

The flip side of this is equally true. Developing strong managerial skills will accelerate your career growth. Organizations depend on good processes and systems, but people are their most valuable resource because it's the people who truly drive the results of any organization. That's why those who are most effective at managing teams of people are the ones most likely to earn the trust of leadership. Once you find yourself in this situation, you are given more opportunities. This further accelerates your learning curve, leading to even more opportunities, which creates a virtuous cycle of rapid career growth. Many large company leadership development programs such as those at Dell and General Electric are a testament to how critical they believe it is to have a deep bench of exceptional managers.

8

There is another virtuous cycle that takes place when you become an outstanding manager. Great people flock to great managers, great people stick with those managers, and great people go above and beyond for those managers. The better your management capabilities are, the more you'll attract and retain great people, and the more all of you will enjoy mutual success as a team. Having great teams puts the wind at your back as you grow and take on new roles.

If you are deeper into your career with lots of management experience, don't let these warnings about embracing these practices early in your career scare you off. Anyone can improve at any stage—it primarily comes down to one's commitment and effort. Don't let your experience level, personality type, or any other factor fool you into thinking you can't become a top-tier manager. Desire is the most important element, followed by your willingness to be honest with yourself about where you need to get better and the steps you have to implement to improve. There isn't a perfect manager out there who has mastered all of the fundamentals. Truly great managers and leaders are those who have committed themselves to a lifelong journey of learning and self-improvement.

What does it mean to be a truly great manager? If you ask people *what it feels like* to work for such a manager, these are some of the things you would likely hear from them:

- They feel respected by the manager.
- They feel encouraged on a regular basis.
- They feel empowered.
- They feel they are continually growing and developing.
- They feel they are compensated fairly from a monetary and emotional perspective.

- They want to go above and beyond for their manager and their team.

When you work for a great manager, that manager makes you feel like they are the coach, you are the player, and you are both doing everything you can to win the game together. The manager is always trying to develop you and the team. You feel like the manager is on your side.

One way to look at this is through the following depiction:

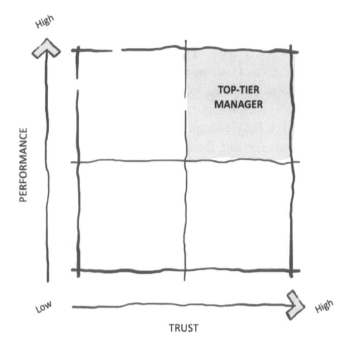

The left dimension is a manager's performance. A high-performing manager is somebody who can drive great results. Employees want to work for a manager who performs because that manager supports the employee's success in their role. This equates to financial reward and career growth for the employee, such as the ability to take on new projects or expanded roles.

The bottom dimension is the trust the manager fosters amongst the team. Employees want to work for a manager they trust because they know the manager will do the right thing and the manager "has their back."

The manager who is low on performance and trust is both ineffective and can't be trusted to put their employees' or the company's interests before their own. This is not the manager anyone aspires to be. This is the type of manager who makes employees run for the hills because this manager doesn't get the job done and the employee doesn't trust this manager to look out for them.

A manager who is high on performance but low on trust is somebody who delivers for the broader organization, but often does so at the expense of their team members. One example of this manager is the successful "ballbuster" who grinds the team, operates in sometimes questionable ways, and likely takes all the credit. Employees may be rewarded and viewed as successful working under this manager, but chances are they become emotionally drained.

A manager who is low on performance but high on trust is somebody teammates know they can trust to do the right thing and they may even enjoy working with that manager as a person. However, they likely do not feel confident the manager is capable of leading their team in the direction of success. It's often the case that people will speak of such a manager as "a good guy" or "a nice woman," and follow that up with "but . . .". Employees working for this type of manager typically do not experience the degree of growth and professional development they desire.

A manager who is in the top right quadrant has the unique blend of performance and character that makes them truly special. Their approach engenders the strongest loyalty amongst their team—people want to work for this person. The team is more likely to win together and to enjoy the journey as well. And the manager is more likely to go places in their career as a result. Make it your mission to be in the top right quadrant and you will not only inspire people to perform and enjoy the fruits of that success, but you will foster lifelong relationships and enjoy your career journey that much more.

In the following chapters, we will dive deep into all of the fundamental characteristics, skills, and tools to support you in your endeavor to become a top-tier manager. Throughout our journey together, one of the most important qualities that will support you on your path is self-awareness.

To that end, now is the perfect opportunity to lay the groundwork with some important self-reflection. One of the best tools for self-reflection is journaling. Writing has been shown time and again to have the power to clarify your thoughts and intentions.

Before reading on, I encourage you to <u>take at least fifteen minutes</u> to reflect on your answers to these questions, ideally by writing down your thoughts and internalizing your responses:

- When it comes to successful management, what do you believe comes naturally to you? What have others told you they think you are particularly good at?

- What do you believe you are going to need to work on the most?
- What makes you the most uncomfortable to work on with respect to your own self-improvement? What do you tend to avoid or deprioritize that could become a barrier for you in reaching your full potential as a manager?
- Who in your mind has been the strongest manager you've worked with and what did you most value about their approach?
- What is your personal definition of success on your journey to reaching your full potential as a manager? Why?

If you took the time to do that, you are off to an excellent start. If you did not, please make sure you do it soon. Honest self-reflection and your intention to learn and grow will serve you well on this path, and without it you are already behind the curve.

The world needs more truly great managers, and it needs them now more than ever. Staggering numbers of people are not as satisfied in their jobs they could be, and time and again studies show one of the top determining factors of job satisfaction is the quality of the manager. We're all waiting for you to lead us to greatness. Let's dive in.

Chapter 2:

The Seven Characteristics

of Great Managers

If you were to ask the average person what comes to mind when they think about being a manager, chances are they might tell you:

"That's the person in charge."

"They're in control and making the decisions."

"They're the one telling other people what to do."

But if you ask somebody to speak about great managers, it's unlikely they would say, "They made all the decisions," or "They were really good at telling people what to do."

That's because exceptional management has little to do with the power or authority inherent in the position. Also, while sound decision-making is critical and a take-charge attitude can be helpful in certain circumstances, we all know these can be taken too far. Knowing when to back off or to go with your team's recommended course of action is just as important. Likewise, effectively tasking people is a valuable skill, but world-class managers build their teams up to the point where their team members are skilled at setting their own priorities.

As you can see, there is much more depth to becoming a great manager than the average person recognizes at first glance. To be high on the dimensions of performance and trust, it's not just what you do that matters—i.e., the tactics and approaches you employ to lead people—it's who you are as a person and how you go about doing those things that sets you apart. To help you become truly exceptional, we will dive into seven essential characteristics of outstanding managers and leaders.

If you want to reach the heights of your potential and become exceptional as a manager, focus on being Transparent, Empathetic, Adaptable, a Clear Communicator, Humble, Empowering, and Responsive. Become a T.E.A.C.H.E.R.

This list is not framed as an acronym simply to be cute or to help you remember the traits. Teaching employees is one of the most crucial roles of a manager. By helping people gain new skills, they become more proficient at their jobs and contribute more to the team and to the organization as a whole. This not only drives results, but it leads to better employee retention, which keeps the organization's most valuable resource—its talent pool—well-stocked. And you are only as strong as the team that supports you. The more you build them up, the better off everyone will be.

In the following sections, we will discuss these characteristics in more depth, explain why they are so crucial, and explore how you can put them into practice. As you will see, while each of the individual characteristics contributes to making you a better manager, it's the combination of all of them together that makes you truly exceptional.

Transparent

Years ago, I was advising the leader of the "new business ventures" arm of a large corporation. His team was responsible for launching and incubating new start-ups. Over the first nine months in his role, this leader and his team launched two new businesses. One concept was showing significant promise, but the second was struggling. As they approached a key checkpoint where the committee making "go/no-go" decisions was likely going to shut the struggling business down, the manager approached me about his predicament.

"I'm in a difficult position," he said. "My team is having trouble coming to terms with the fact that the business they are working on isn't going to be viable. They want to go into the go/no-go meeting in two weeks with a request for three more months of funding so they can modify the business model one more time. But when I sat down with the head of the committee to see what his thoughts were, he told me the committee has already formed a strong view that the time has come to shut this one down. I haven't shared this information with my team because I'm worried it will be too demoralizing given how much work they're putting into the upcoming presentation. I was thinking about letting events take their course and allowing the committee to communicate their recommendation in the meeting."

"Do you think your team sees this outcome coming at all?" I asked.

"Yes, but they're so worried about being a part of something that failed that they are still fighting for it. They are worried about losing their jobs. They don't need to be as worried as they are because we'll end up redeploying them on a new project or role, but it's a tough pill for them to swallow since they're all such high achievers and they're not used to experiencing failure."

"Have you told them they don't need to worry about their jobs?" I asked.

"No, I haven't wanted to say anything that might send a signal about their business not moving forward until the time was right."

It was clear to me as the objective outsider that this manager was expressing genuine concern for his team. But his chosen approach was not what was in his teammates' best interests. By shielding his team from the news and failing to communicate in an open and honest way, he was at risk of eroding their trust. And because he was considering letting them expend another two weeks of hard work and emotional energy on a futile proposal, he risked lost productivity and further frustration among his team. In short, he was not embodying the first key characteristics of great managers:

Be transparent.

The spirit of being transparent was articulated well by the CEO of Digital Equipment Corporation who, when asked about the most important values he wished to see embraced by his organization, replied: "Let's be open, honest, trusting, and trusted by our customers, our suppliers, and each other."

Being open and honest creates an environment of trust and credibility. It shows people you are authentic and you have integrity, which are two essential ingredients of true collaboration. It also paves the way for mutual understanding and respect, which are especially crucial in situations where there are differences between people in their views, interests, or needs.

When it comes to the people reporting to you, transparency shows employees you have their best interests in mind. When you are forthright with information, it invites necessary dialog with your teammates and opens the door for them to share their thoughts and opinions. This helps them, but it makes you better as well. When everyone is working from the same information and context, and when you're able to effectively tap into your team for their points of view, this fosters better decision-making across your whole team. But when you withhold information, you open the floodgates for more questions and emails, wasted time, and poor decision-making.

Transparency also promotes a healthy work environment by reducing the opportunity for interpersonal issues and drama to capture people's attention and draw focus away from work. An employee wondering, "Why wasn't I invited to that meeting?" is a simple but common example of this type of unnecessary distraction.

The higher the stakes, the more critical transparency becomes. For example, a large public company was going through a period of poor financial performance that required them to reduce headcount. Rumors circulated about impending layoffs. While nearly everybody knew layoffs were coming, company leadership did not provide honest answers to questions about the situation that came up during town hall meetings. They reasoned that sharing too much would create turmoil among employees and would drive talented individuals to leave the organization. But choosing to remain silent did not reduce the turmoil anyway, and once the layoffs took place and people's fears were confirmed, leadership had lost significant trust among the employee base due to their lack of transparency.

But what about situations that involve sensitive or confidential information? Of course, there may be times where it is either not possible or not prudent to be fully transparent. But such examples are exceedingly rare. In general, managers and organizations aren't as transparent as they should be. They pay lip service to it, but they consistently miss opportunities to build trust through transparency.

Ray Dalio, the founder of Bridgewater Associates, the largest hedge fund in the world, once discussed the importance of transparency using the example of a company on the verge of being sold. This is one of the most extreme examples of something the majority of companies deem to be confidential. Most companies attempt to keep knowledge of a potential acquisition hidden from the employee base until the last possible minute. But Dalio advised that even in a situation like this, it is better for a company to be open with employees rather than to try to keep it quiet. After all, the news will eventually come to light, and the damage done by not being transparent almost always outweighs the risks of sharing the truth about the situation with openness and honesty.

The principle of transparency is so foundational that it's the basis of the book *Radical Candor* (St. Martin's Press, 2017) by Kim Scott. In this book, Scott says that people are too afraid to challenge each other in candid conversation, and she champions the many benefits of calling it like it is. It's important to note that Scott recommends balancing this with humility, kindness and an orientation toward helping everyone develop and succeed. Otherwise candid conversation can become imbalanced and even aggressive, which destroys the benefits of direct communication.

Be as clear, direct, open, and honest as you can, and your team, your peers, and your bosses will all respect you for it. Do this in as many ways as you can—whether it's discussing company plans or it's talking about your own thoughts and motivations. Transparency disarms people and fosters strong relationships. And because most people find it difficult to be transparent, doing so immediately sets you apart from the vast majority of people in a good way.

Without question, the best managers are transparent. If you want to be a great manager, learning to be transparent is the first principle to embrace.

Putting it into practice:

- Make it your default mindset to be "transparent first," and force yourself to have very strong arguments for when not to be open and forthright, rather than the other way around.
- Tell your employees you will be as open as possible, follow through on that commitment, and ask your employees to reciprocate by being as open as possible with you.
- Always be as upfront as you can about what you are doing and why, and make sure your transparent communication reaches all levels of employees who report up through you.
- A big part of transparency is simply about ensuring people have appropriate context. Err on the side of being inclusive when inviting people to meetings and trust that they can balance their own time and make the right decision about whether to attend. (It can help to clarify when meetings are optional and to provide as much detail as possible about the meeting in advance to help an employee make the right call regarding their attendance.)
- Copy people on emails when they are helping with the work related to that email, which will further ensure employees have as much context as possible.
- Try not to hide anything from your employees. Likewise, don't hide things from your own

manager. Model the behavior you would like to see in your employees when working with your own manager.

- Avoid becoming involved in any political games, which is one of the surest ways to lose the trust of people around you (including people who are not directly involved in the situation).

Empathetic

Do you recall the story of United Airlines' tremendous public relations gaffe surrounding a physician who was dragged off of a plane from his paid seat to make room for an employee?

The CEO, Oscar Munoz, issued a statement saying, "I apologize for having to re-accommodate these customers," for which he experienced significant blowback.

His second statement compounded the error when he blamed the victim—describing the passenger as defiant, belligerent, and disruptive.

It was only on his third try that the company was able to move forward in the public eye when he said, "I promise you we will do better."

This example illustrates a number of obvious gaps in effective leadership, but the one that stood out the most in the public perception was Munoz's seeming inability to understand the customer's point of view in a situation like this. This understanding of another person's point of view is the essence of our next essential characteristic of successful managers—empathy.

Every employee, including you, wants to be heard, understood, and valued. It is one of the most basic human needs we have and it's crucial in team environments. Great managers fulfill this need with their team members on a daily basis. And they do it by being empathetic.

What is empathy?

Very simply, displaying empathy means that you are able to place yourself in another person's shoes, to understand how another person may be thinking and feeling, and to use this knowledge to act and to make decisions in a way that is optimal for all parties.

But as simple as it sounds, it is one of the most under-expressed and undervalued traits in leadership. While some of this can be explained by selection mechanisms that focus far too exclusively on a person's results and on not enough on the leadership characteristics they embody as they deliver those results, there is more to the story.

A big part of why empathy is underrepresented as a trait is that it is misunderstood. People incorrectly think of it as a "touchy-feely" trait that is only about making people feel good. Not surprisingly, this view of empathy doesn't align with many people's perception of strong leadership, so they don't pay sufficient attention to it and they fail to work on developing their own capacity for empathy.

But this idea misses the mark completely. Empathy is a foundational component of success among leaders. In fact, many experts and leaders alike believe it to be the single most important leadership trait.

Why is empathy so important?

It comes back to where we began. The best leaders—the strongest managers—are high on the dimension of trust and performance. Empathy contributes directly to both of these dimensions.

Let's begin with trust.

There is simply no better way to cultivate trust in professional relationships than to demonstrate a sympathetic understanding of the other person's situation and point of view. When a person believes they are truly heard and understood, they feel respected and they trust that you will treat them in a manner that is honest, ethical, and fair. They return that respect. Not only that, but they are so much more likely to go above and beyond for you. And they are more likely to see you as approachable, so they will surface issues more openly and promptly, allowing you to resolve challenges with greater speed and effectiveness.

Empathy is foundational to trust. Without sufficient empathy, you cannot cultivate trusting relationships and teams. Excel at empathy, and you will position yourself to have a high-functioning, effective team.

Empathy also contributes directly to the dimension of performance. A significant portion of the decisions you make as a manager are people-related decisions. Empathy is a skill that improves your ability to make good decisions because you are better able to see all points of view and understand the potential impact of your decisions on people. Success as a manager depends upon effective decision-making.

This extends beyond your team to other teams and functions in the organization, to third parties and partners, and to customers. Whether it's collaborating with other people, or it's negotiating, or it's serving customers, just about everything you and your team do is enhanced through the skill of empathy.

Calling empathy a "skill" naturally raises a question, and it's one of the most common questions I field when coaching individuals, teams, and organizations:

Can empathy be learned or is it an innate trait?

In my experience, the answer is clearly "both." Like most skills, some people are more naturally inclined to possess the skill, but it can also be developed with intention and practice.

So how do you practice empathy?

The question itself raises the biggest challenge with respect to the cultivation of empathy. For it to be real empathy, it needs to be genuine and authentic. We've all been on the receiving end of calculated behaviors that were motivated by the other person's self-interests. And chances are things didn't work out in that person's favor. It's easy for us as humans to spot ulterior motives or a lack of genuine intentions. Such efforts usually backfire, leading to a loss of trust.

This is one of the reasons empathy is such a rare trait, especially in leadership roles. The only way to embody empathy is to genuinely place other people's concerns at the same level as your own (and often above your own), whether it's a teammate, a colleague, a partner, or a customer.

Most of us do genuinely care about the needs of other people, and that alone is sufficient basis for the cultivation of empathy. The rest can be practiced.

The simplest way to build your empathetic ability is also the most direct. All you need to do is consciously ask yourself this question as often as possible: "How would I feel in this situation if I were in that person's shoes?"

This works because, as people, we are more alike than we are different, and more often than not, your answer to that question is likely to be similar to theirs.

Over time, and especially as you get to know a person and their unique qualities, you can take empathy a step further by asking yourself, "How do they likely feel in this situation?" To be able to answer this accurately requires having a complete understanding of where that individual is coming from. It forces you to step out of your perspective and truly adopt theirs, incorporating what you know about them as a person and what is unique about their side of the situation.

When it's appropriate, you can just ask another person where they are coming from. You don't need to be a mind-reader. In fact, your interest in them and your willingness to listen are already a demonstration of empathy.

There's no need to overcomplicate this process. Consistently put yourself in other people's shoes before you respond, make decisions, or take any other action. Consider what they must be thinking or feeling. Recall a time you were in a similar situation and how you felt. And when it comes time to act, do your best to place other people's concerns on the same level as your own.

Beyond that, it's helpful to be conscious of the biggest barrier to the cultivation of empathy: the reflexive tendency for our minds to jump back to thinking about ourselves first, whether it's arguing our point of view, defending ourselves, focusing on what we want, or any number of other self-focused responses. We don't need to try to squelch all of these; just notice them and redirect attention toward seeking to understand the other person's perspective first. After that, we are more likely to balance our point of view with theirs and arrive at the best course of action.

If you commit yourself to these simple approaches, you will undoubtedly become a more effective manager. That goes for anyone, regardless of his or her starting point on the spectrum of empathy.

Putting it into practice:

- Seek to understand other people first. Ask yourself the question, "How would I feel if I were in their shoes?" This is especially important to do before giving feedback, which is one of the most critical times to ensure you are demonstrating a high degree of empathy.
- Practice listening before speaking as often as possible.
- Try not to default to lecturing or dictating. Rely on asking questions (i.e., "Why?" or Socratic dialog) to help guide team members to the ideal course of action.
- Keep a pulse on what is going on with your team both at work and outside of work so that you can better understand their personal and professional situations.
- Schedule regular one-on-ones with your team where the focus is on their professional development and how they are doing rather than exclusively on task-focused catch-ups.

- Get to know your team members on a personal level.

Adaptable

One of the essential takeaways from Darwin's work on evolution is that the survival of a species depends less on its strength or intelligence than on its ability to adapt to its changing environment. In a matter as central to a species as its very survival, this ability to change in productive ways ranks above all else.

In recent history, a similar idea has been promoted regarding organizations. As the pace of change in most markets has increased and the threat of disruption looms in unexpected places, an organization's ability to adapt has been called the new competitive advantage.

The same principle applies to the individual, making adaptability our third essential characteristic of great managers.

Employers are increasingly in search of managers who are highly adaptable, and for obvious reasons. These managers are more open to new ideas. They are able to learn faster and mobilize quickly in new situations. They drive greater productivity through their orientation toward improving things rather than defaulting to, "That's the way things have always been done." They can adjust on the fly when things don't go according to plan without resorting to panic. All of these traits make them more effective at their jobs and more versatile. As a result, they are able to be put into a wider variety of leadership roles, including being placed in stretch roles and being put in charge of areas in which they may not have significant proven expertise.

This is why, in a survey of human resources leaders conducted by Right Management and detailed in The Flux Report (2014), over 90 percent of respondents indicated that the ability of a candidate to adapt to change and to deal with uncertainty will become even more of a top recruitment goal in the future.

One of the most important aspects of adaptability for a manager is the ability to tailor one's management style to people's differing work styles.

As an example, some people are comfortable with ambiguity and like being given space to run, and they will seek the guidance of their manager only when they need it. Others prefer structure and clearly defined tasks. If a manager is too hands-on with the first type of person, that individual may feel suffocated and become frustrated. Likewise, if a manager is too hands-off with the second type of person, that individual may feel lost and uncomfortable.

We each have different needs which are shaped by our personalities, our unique strengths and weaknesses, and our work styles. These requirements also change over time based on our development trajectory. For example, our need for hands-on management goes down as we come up the learning curve in a role. The truly effective manager is tuned into an employee's needs and is capable of adapting as the situation dictates.

It turns out that this is rarer than you might think. It's common for managers to be comfortable with a certain management style and to default to working with everybody using that approach.

Take micromanagers as an example. Micromanagers are hyper-involved in the details of people's work and they struggle to give people adequate freedom. This can be frustrating for anyone, but particularly for the employee who is highly competent and autonomous.

The other important aspect of being adaptable is being appropriately flexible. This is often one of the earliest challenges people face as they transition from individual contributor to manager.

As an individual contributor, you have control over how you do things (provided you don't work for a micromanager). Your level of control and autonomy tends to grow over time as you gain experience, and it's common for it to be at its peak in your role as an individual contributor at the very point you are promoted and become a manager. Now, as a manager, you have to let go of a meaningful portion of that control to your team members as they execute on the work. This can be a difficult thing to do for many people, particularly if you are someone who places a high standard on the quality of your work. As a manager, the people you are overseeing may not be not as skilled at doing the work as you are. After all, that disparity may be a big reason why you were promoted to the position you are in.

This is where flexibility comes into play. Adaptable managers are open to going with other people's approaches and perspectives, even if it might not be the way they would choose to do things. They see that there is more than one way to get the job done. And they recognize the importance of giving team members enough freedom and power to make their own choices, even if that sometimes means allowing them to go with a less-than-ideal approach.

Being flexible and adjusting your managerial approach to the particular individual and situation helps ensure you get the best out of your team. When you've mastered these skills, you avoid lost productivity because of employees who are spinning their wheels as a result of insufficient guidance. You also optimize your team's learning and professional growth by providing the right level and type of guidance based on each person's needs. Adaptability naturally contributes to high performance and trust.

Like our other characteristics, adaptability is a muscle that can be built through exercise.

Putting it into practice:

- Begin by recognizing that nobody has the perfect managerial style—everyone can improve.
- Determine where each of your employees are on their development trajectory in their role. Devote more time to training, coaching and providing feedback to those who are coming up the learning curve.
- Assess each employee's working style and employ managerial tactics that align with that style. We will discuss this more in a later chapter. It never hurts to ask your employees how they prefer to be managed (but you don't necessarily need to adapt to every preference).
- Accept that in most situations where you are delegating work, your job is to coach and refine rather than to change or redo a team member's work.
- When team members come with ideas or proposals, keep an open mind. Be wary of saying "no" too much.

- Don't provide all the answers to your team members. Leave things open for them to figure out. Be comfortable leaving a meeting without having everything nailed down if it fosters greater learning and independence among your team members.

Clear Communicator

"If you want me to speak for an hour, I am ready today. If you want me to speak for just a few minutes, it will take me a few weeks to prepare."
—Woodrow Wilson

After analyzing thousands of employee surveys from companies of all sizes, I have found one element most shapes employee opinions of their organizations and their managers—communication. Solid communication is an essential ingredient of effective teams and well-functioning organizations. And the bar for effective communication is climbing as companies globalize, whether that means overcoming linguistic barriers, communicating in a way that transcends cultural differences across offices, or simply keeping up with the pace of communication required in any large or distributed organization.

Clear communication is a must if you're going to become a top-tier manager. Solid communication is foundational to every aspect of your role. It's the means by which you convey the organization's strategy to your team and how you connect your team's objectives to the bigger picture. It's how you convey your goals, objectives and expectations. It's how you delegate tasks. It's how you coach and deliver feedback. It's how you recognize people and motivate them. It's how you collaborate across functions. There's nothing communication ability doesn't touch.

The importance of clear communication probably seems obvious to you. But there's a reason it's so common for communication to be raised as an issue on employee opinion surveys. It's difficult terrain to master.

For starters, it encompasses so many forms—in-person interactions, videoconferencing, phone calls, emails, texts and direct messages, formal presentations, slide decks, memos and prose deliverables, analyses and charts, the list goes on. We all have strengths and weaknesses with respect to how effectively we communicate, yet most of us are required to communicate through most or all of these modalities, regardless of whether it happens to play to our particular strengths.

On top of this, you have to tailor your communication to the individuals involved or adapt your approach based on the situation. This becomes even trickier when you consider that we all take in information differently. Even if you communicate something clearly, there's a good chance somebody may misunderstand or misinterpret your intended message. As a manager and a leader, you increasingly see that it doesn't matter where a communication breakdown happens; instead, you recognize the need to judge the success of your communication based on how effectively it is received (and in many cases, how effectively it is cascaded to others without being distorted in a game of telephone). In other words, the recipients' perception becomes your reality, which places the onus squarely on you.

As if this weren't challenging enough, you need to communicate with the right frequency. This almost always means *more*. It's rare that we over-communicate. But it's very easy to fall short. Frequent, effective communication takes time. Often it takes time we don't feel we have as busy managers.

So how do we improve on this important characteristic of clear communication?

Begin by ensuring that you choose the best mode of communication for the situation, taking into consideration your objective, who you are communicating to, how they best consume information like this, and so forth. Is this a situation where a conversation is best, or will a quick email suffice? Should the conversation be in-person? Should you limit who is a part of the discussion? Is it an informal discussion or is it important to prepare materials to ensure the discussion flows a certain way? Do you need charts or visuals to help the person digest data, or images or videos to better convey the emotional impact of a message?

There is no formula for answering questions like these, but strong managers build their intuition through experience and are thoughtful about how they approach communication.

In certain cases, organizations have recognized the situational effectiveness of various forms of communication and they have embedded specific recommendations or requirements into how they operate. For example, Amazon does not allow employees to use PowerPoint/slide presentations when communicating strategy. Instead, they require people to write strategy documents in the form of a memo. The reason for this is that prose forces a higher degree of clarity in logic and flow. Amazon has found that this company norm improves people's quality of thinking and decision-making.

This is the time to take into account your own strengths and weaknesses with respect to communication channels and to balance them against the other considerations.

Several years ago, while working at General Electric, I reported to a manager who was not an effective communicator over email. Her emails tended to be terse and she didn't take the time to provide sufficient explanation. But when she gave in-person feedback, she took the time to clarify issues and always showed that she cared. Surprisingly, despite her clear strengths when managing in an in-person situation, she almost always opted to work remotely and encouraged others to do the same. This decision did not play to her strengths and the team's productivity clearly suffered because of this approach.

Once you have determined the best modality and communication approach for a given situation, take the time to clarify your communication objective.

What does success look like in this situation?

To help define success for yourself, you can use the following questions as a helpful frame:

What do you want the other person(s) to *know?*

What do you want the other person(s) to *feel?*

What do you want the other person(s) to *do?*

After taking the time to clarify your objective and define success (a process that does not always need to take significant time and can become intuitive and automatic in many situations with practice), it's time to move to executing your communication.

How do you improve your effectiveness in executing your communication?

First, communicate *more*. This is a piece of generic advice that likely applies to just about everyone.

Second, *prepare*. I can't stress enough how far a little preparation can take you, especially with respect to any form of verbal communication. Outline points that you need to convey in a conversation and bring notes for yourself. Practice the words you'll choose when articulating something that requires sensitivity. Rehearse a presentation over and over in advance until you're comfortable you can deliver it to the best of your ability.

Third, *practice*. Any skill can be enhanced through intentional practice. If you're a weak writer, sign up for a class in written communication. If you're not a good presenter because you're afraid of public speaking, sign up for a workshop or join Toastmasters. If you struggle speaking off-the-cuff when facilitating meetings, try taking an improv class.

Fourth, *listen*. Communication should virtually always be a two-way interaction. Listen more than you speak. Ask questions. It's important that the other people feel heard, but that's also your vehicle for understanding how well your communication is being understood. Listening is a skill just like anything else, and it can also be practiced.

And lastly, remember that one of the most overlooked aspects of in-person communication is the importance of non-verbal communication. Your body language, energy level, and tone say more to the other person/people than your words. And you guessed it, non-verbal communication can also be practiced just like all the other aspects of communication.

Putting it into practice:

- Communicate constantly. It's almost impossible to over-communicate. Don't wait for the questions to come in; make it your goal to preempt as many questions as you can.
- Keep your door open as often as possible. Give your employees the freedom to come in spontaneously with questions.
- Determine other people's preferred communication channels based on the situation (e.g., in person, phone, email) and try to lean on using the ones that are most effective with them.
- Likewise, determine your own strengths (e.g., written, verbal, phone, in-person, etc.) and play to those strengths while proactively working on improving in your areas of weakness (e.g., if writing is not a strength, consider taking a writing course).
- Prepare and practice before you communicate. This can assist you with clarity and brevity. It's commonly the case that, rather than speaking off the cuff, the best communicators organize their thoughts ahead of time and practice what they are going to say.
- Foster communication among your employees by asking them questions.
- Talk to your team on a daily basis. If there isn't anything in particular you need to discuss, don't shy away from non-work-related topics. This

fosters an open communication forum between you and your team and can often trigger questions or topics neither of you had thought of until you were in the moment.

Humble

Teddy Roosevelt famously said, "The best executive is the one who has sense enough to pick good men to do what he wants done, and self-restraint enough to keep from meddling with them while they do it."

But these days, we have come to expect our business leaders to be brash, outspoken, arrogant individuals. It's as though we believe on some level that those traits are necessary to survive as a leader, or at the very least that they come as a package deal with strong leadership capability.

This couldn't be further from the truth. Arrogance is always a weakness, even if it takes time to catch up with some people. We all know stories of leaders whose egos eventually became their downfall. And while some are able to succeed in spite of their egos, we'll never know how much more successful they might have been had it not been for their arrogance.

The best leaders—the ones with the deepest and most profound impact on those around them and the ones who have contributed the most to the lasting success of organizations—are humble.

In a study on successful CEOs in *Administrative Science Quarterly*, humility was directly correlated with empowered employees, a key driver of the success of their companies. As the study explained, "Humble people willingly seek accurate self-knowledge and accept their imperfections while remaining fully aware of their talents and abilities. They appreciate others' positive worth, strengths, and contributions and thus have no need for entitlement or dominance over others."

As a manager of people, humility directly translates into better decision-making. A humble manager does not need to be right. They place a higher value on what is true than on their opinion, and they would rather come to the right answer than worry about their sense of pride or their need to exercise authority.

As Arron Grow of the School of Applied Leadership at the City University of Seattle says, "Many leaders want to control everything. But some things can't be known up front or beforehand. You have to know when to take charge—and when to let go and not try to force everything to go your way. Sometimes, it's important to admit that you don't know the best answer and wait until you have the best information to make a decision or change."

A humble manager is also willing to take this a step further and admit when they are wrong. "When you're willing to share your own missteps, and how you dealt with and recovered from them, you earn trust from your team," Grow says. This is another way of saying "be accountable," and it can be one of the strongest ways of building trust and loyalty among your team and with your peers and superiors.

And because such a manager is willing to place themselves on the same plane as everyone around them, they are more in touch with people's needs. This translates into a competitive advantage. Kevin Brogan, Vice President of Meadows Casino, puts it this way: "The best managers are those who have an intimate knowledge of the needs of both their customers and their employees."

While it may at first seem strange to discuss ways in which you can practice humility, this essential characteristic of great managers shares commonality with being empathetic. It can be practiced and developed, but it takes a certain amount of willingness. Not everyone has this willingness. Some people's egos are too strong to allow for such a change to take place. It may take a powerful event or circumstance to humble those people before they are willing to see themselves in a new, less superior light.

But most of us recognize we aren't perfect and are willing to admit our weaknesses. And that alone is enough of a foundation upon which to practice humility. Every bit of effort you put into it will pay dividends, sometimes in unexpected ways.

Putting it into practice:

- Engage in self-reflection. One of the most powerful tools is to write in a journal—chronicle what you did well during the day and what you could have handled better. As Confucius said, "By three methods we may learn wisdom: First, by reflection, which is noblest; Second, by imitation, which is easiest; and third by experience, which is the bitterest."
- Ask for input frequently from your team. Remember that people want to work for managers who value their opinions.

- Admit mistakes. It's difficult to admit when you mess up, but doing so only increases people's respect for you.
- Accept that you don't have all the answers. Get comfortable with ambiguity.
- Know when to take charge and when to let go.
- Don't force everything to go your way.
- If someone can be trusted, back off and let them do their job. Don't micromanage.
- Don't worry if some of this doesn't come easily to you at first. Like all valuable characteristics, it may take time, and the most important component to growth is your intention and effort.

Empowering

In the opening chapter we discussed how the shift from being an individual contributor to a manager is such a significant one because your individual success is now dictated by the success of your team rather than by your own solitary contributions.

As a manager, you aren't supposed to be doing everyone else's jobs, of course, or you wouldn't have a team. Yet many new managers struggle with relaxing control. It's a common mistake for a new manager to try to be everywhere, approving every decision, and overseeing every work product, rather than shifting their focus toward building and growing an outstanding team.

When observing managers who take on more expansive roles over time and comparing them with those who do not, one of the primary differences is the degree to which managers empower their teams.

There is a straightforward reason for this: leverage. The more involved you need to be in the day-to-day tasks of each of your team member's jobs, the less you are able to focus on the aspects that are unique to your leadership role, such as setting the direction for your group, working with your peers, and managing up. Micromanagement of subordinates also limits your bandwidth for taking on additional responsibilities and it reduces the organization's confidence in your ability to handle managing larger teams—especially big leadership positions that require managing other managers.

It's been said by many leadership experts that empowering other people not only goes hand-in-hand with great leadership, but empowering other people *is* great leadership. Laszlo Bock, Google's SVP of People Operations, explained it this way: "Your end goal is what can we do together to problem-solve. I've contributed my piece, and then I step back."

As a manager, "your piece" in the problem-solving equation may be smaller than you realize. It's common for employees to come to you with problems and look for you to solve them. But your job is not to solve all the problems your team members present to you. Your piece is to break down barriers that stand in the way of your employees being successful—in other words, the problems they truly cannot solve on their own. Each time you solve a problem that they might be able to solve themselves, they become more dependent on you (i.e., less empowered), and an opportunity is missed for their growth and development. When a problem is raised to you, it's useful to identify which of four types it is:

1. Is the employee simply venting about something with no solution? While a little bit of occasional venting happens, it's best to respond to their venting with the question, "Is there any action either of us can take to help improve the situation?" (This is usually enough to help someone realize they are spending time on an unproductive thread. Over time, it retrains people to focus on positive action rather than venting negativity.)

2. Is it a problem the employee can solve on their own? Turn the question back around on them and ask them what they think would be the best way to solve it.

3. Is it a problem the employee can solve on their own with some coaching from you? Ask them how they might solve it, but offer some suggestions to nudge them in the right direction, and coach them through the problem-solving process.

4. Is it a problem that truly requires you to help solve it? Take action and break down the barrier!

As an example, suppose a team member comes to you needing some important information from another group in the organization.

This is clearly not an employee venting (#1), so you might begin by asking them who they have gone to so far to seek out the information. If they tell you nobody, then try asking who they think might be the best person to reach out to for the information (#2). If they aren't sure who to go to, progress a step further and offer a little more support. Give them suggestions for who might have the information they need, but let them take it from there if possible (#3). But suppose you learn that they already went to the appropriate person and were denied, so they need you to connect with that person's manager to help break down the barrier. Then step in and do so (#4).

The point this illustration is attempting to convey is to try not to exceed the amount of support you need to provide in a situation so you can maximize how much your teammate learns and how much independence they gain over time.

This is not to be misinterpreted as a reluctance to help, and it takes some art to ensure your approach comes across in the appropriate way to your team members. You want to offer as much help as you can. But as a manager, the best help you can provide in a given situation is to use it as an opportunity to build an employee's own problem-solving skills, to guide them toward increasing levels of independence and autonomy, and where necessary, to step in to swiftly tackle those barriers that only you can break down.

Empowering an employee is the most potent way to promote their learning and development. We all learn best through direct experience. By giving your team members the appropriate degree of autonomy and responsibility, you stretch them beyond their current capability and stimulate professional growth. It is certainly possible to swing too far in this direction and "give too much rope," but great managers learn how to strike the right balance with each of their employees and empower them to take on as much as they can handle.

Empowerment is both a mindset and a set of practical behaviors.

Putting it into practice:

- Remember that the more hands-off you are able to be with an employee, the better it is for both you and your team member.
- Know when to take charge and when to let go. Let people do their jobs.
- Don't jump immediately to solving problems team members present to you. Turn it around and help them work through the problem-solving process, stepping in to break down barriers when it's appropriate.
- Seek input from team members and involve them in decisions beyond their scope of responsibility so they gain exposure to thinking through bigger problems and grow as a result.
- Give people stretch assignments.
- In a situation where you are introducing one of your team members to others they will be working with for the first time, position your employee in the most elevated way you can based on what is reasonable for their role and experience level. It's common for people to prefer to talk to or work with the most senior person they can. If they default to wanting to work with you, this limits the opportunity for your team member to grow and reduces your leverage.
- If possible, identify a potential successor for yourself and spend extra effort coaching and empowering that person to take on more responsibility over time. Sometimes great managers are temporarily held back from taking on new roles

because their current role is too critical and there isn't a ready backfill.

Responsive

It's been said that a person's success is determined by three traits—availability, affability, and ability—in decreasing order of importance. While it's a bit tongue-in-cheek, it contains an often-overlooked truth: It doesn't matter if you're the greatest talent that ever lived, you have to be there when you're needed if you're going to be of any value.

That is the spirit of the seventh characteristic of great managers—responsiveness. It's a trait we value in everyone with whom we work, not just managers. But it's especially critical if you want to be among the top tier of managers.

As a manager, a big part of your job is setting priorities, delegating work to team members, and following up on that work. Along the way, team members get stuck and reach out to you for support. If they get what they need quickly, they'll be back on track. But if they're waiting for you because you're too busy, they will slow down or come to a stop until you're available to help them.

This is why responsiveness is so essential to the productivity of your team. By being responsive, you set the tone for action among your team and you are less likely to be the bottleneck for things getting done.

As an example, take the situation where your team member has finished a draft of a deliverable. Let's assume it is their top priority and they are awaiting feedback from you. Every hour that goes by without you responding to them is an hour of lost productivity on their top priority. Effective managers learn to subordinate their own work—whether that's responding to emails, returning phone calls, or working on their own deliverables—to provide support to their team members first whenever possible. That means they focus first on delegating, getting team members going on tasks, and responding to questions to help get their team members back on track with tasks before they turn their attention back to their individual priorities. This ensures their team members are productive as much as possible, rather than sitting idly or filling time with lower-priority work.

Responsiveness also contributes directly to building trust among a team. It is a way to demonstrate respect for your employees, one of the foundational elements of being a strong manager. People are more motivated to go above and beyond when they work for a manager who demonstrates respect for them.

Being responsive also sets up a positive feedback loop—when employees know they'll get a timely response, they are more likely to reach out to you with questions or issues, fostering the right level of open communication that is the hallmark of the most successful teams.

Although a straightforward characteristic, it's easy to underestimate the impact that a greater degree of responsiveness can have on your effectiveness as a manager.

Putting it into practice:

- Make it a priority to give your employees the time they deserve.

- If you don't have time to provide a full response, it's better to provide an immediate response and tell that person when you will get back to them. (Even a quick note such as "I received your email. I'll review tonight and get back to you tomorrow morning," tells an employee the ball is in your court and it takes the stress off of them.)
- Provide your team with guidelines around using various communication methods, such as which circumstances are best to call/email/text and expected response times for each of those methods. As an example, you might tell employees you will respond to emails within 48 hours but that they should text if they need a response that day.
- Similarly, try to communicate your availability and schedule so people know when to expect your responsiveness to dip due to the demands of your calendar.

The seven characteristics in summary

Be a T.E.A.C.H.E.R. and you have meaningfully set yourself apart as a manager. If you are transparent, empathetic, adaptable, a clear communicator, humble, empowering and responsive, you exude natural leadership competency. Managers who embody these characteristics build the strongest teams, and the ability to build and grow outstanding teams is the number one attribute organizations look for when filling higher-level leadership roles.

As we dive into the next chapters, remember that these seven characteristics are the foundation for outstanding management. Whether it's setting priorities, delegating, hiring, delivering a performance review, or any other job of a manager, it's important that these seven characteristics permeate everything you do. Everyone has their relative strengths and weaknesses as a manager, and we can all improve on any dimension by implementing the practices. Embrace self-reflection as often as you can and make it your consistent practice to improve on these dimensions in everything you do. This will firmly establish you on the path to greatness as a manager.

Chapter 3:

Setting Goals and

Expectations for Your Team

The success of an organization, a team, or an individual depends on the consistent achievement of goals. The goals we set are quite literally the benchmark upon which we measure our success. If we meet or exceed expectations, we're winning. If we fall short, we're losing.

But goals themselves are inherently subjective. Suppose someone who never runs woke up one day and said, "I am going to train for the next month so I can run a mile in under four minutes." If, when the big day came, they clocked a mile in five minutes and they went home feeling crushed by their defeat, I certainly wouldn't share their view that they had failed. The problem was the goal itself, since breaking a four-minute mile is a feat only truly great runners achieve with a lot more than one month of training.

This may seem like an unrealistic example, but a similar scenario happens in organizations all the time. Companies will set grandiose financial targets and come up drastically short. Leaders will commit to unreasonable deadlines. Individuals will take their first job out of school with the expectation that they'll be running a division within three years. The flip side is also common, such as project managers sandbagging their timelines, or sales leaders setting targets their teams will blow out of the water even if they only show up to work two days a week.

As a stark example of poor goal setting, Chris Zook's book *Profit from the Core* (HBR Press, 2010) highlights that when setting growth goals beyond their core business, companies only achieve the goals 8 percent of the time.

Zig Ziglar once wisely said, "A goal properly set is halfway reached." Because of the subjectivity involved in the process, there is an art and science to setting goals, and it's one of the most important skills for a manager to master. But the typical manager spends very little time focused on the act of establishing properly set goals.

A goal that is properly set is one that supports achieving the best possible results of an individual, a team, and an organization. It establishes the marker of success for an individual or a team in a way that everyone can agree upon. It aligns with and ties into the broader objectives of a team or organization, making it clear to people how their effort supports the success of the team or organization. It is motivating and pushes people to perform at their optimal ability, but it doesn't overstretch them or burn them out.

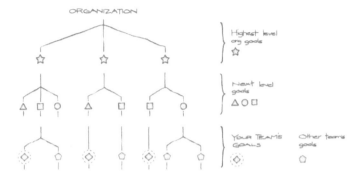

It is critical to understand how your team's goals fit with the broader organization to ensure everyone is positioned to succeed.

As a manager, your first order of business is making sure you and every person on your team have well-defined goals that are written down and mutually agreed upon. You want to be in a position where you could lay out every single one of your teammates' goals and say to yourself, "Yes, if we achieved every one of these things—and we genuinely believe that's well within our reach—we will be successful as a team in our own eyes, in the eyes of my manager, and in the eyes of the broader organization."

Because goals are such an essential element to driving employee performance, it's crucial that the employee be bought into those goals. It's for this reason that the best approach to goal setting is to have your team members take the lead in writing down their own goals, while you play the role of providing feedback and suggesting refinements until the goals are optimally defined. To help guide your team and ensure their goals plug into your broader objectives, it can be helpful to share a version of your own goals with them. The more transparent you are able to be, the better the results you tend to see in the quality of their goals and the degree to which they align with yours. Likewise, if you make them aware that their goals will be shared up the chain with your manager, it drives home the importance of cascading, mutually reinforcing goals.

When establishing goals for an employee, there are three categories to focus on: mission, performance and development.

Mission

At the highest level, it is valuable to begin with having the employee define their mission in one to three sentences. An employee's mission is simply what they have been hired to do—it communicates their major responsibilities as well as their highest-level objective(s) over the next 12 to 24 months.

As an example, a mission statement may read: "As call center manager, my mission is to manage the call-center team of 10 individuals and drive 20 percent improvement in wait time, calls/day/rep, and overall customer satisfaction within two years." Another example is, "As a product manager, my mission is to manage the ABC line of products, growing revenue by 10 percent and margins by 15 percent by collaborating with sales, marketing, supply chain, and manufacturing."

The reason it is so helpful to begin with the employee's mission is because it establishes their overall purpose in simple language. This guides goal setting and keeps people focused on the big picture. If done effectively, it answers two key questions that gauge an employee's success in their role: "What were you brought in to achieve?" and "Were you successful in achieving it?"

Performance goals

Performance goals are what most people think about when it comes to goal setting on the job. Performance goals establish the specific results the employee is responsible for achieving over a given time frame. It's common for employees to have several performance goals, often revolving around specific projects they are working on. Examples of performance goals include:

Role	Performance Goal
Sales Rep	Meet annual revenue target of $500,000 in product sales.
Engineer	Complete design of component X within 6 months, meeting all cost and quality targets for the project.
Marketer	Successfully execute marketing campaign by September 30 that drives 1,000+ new customer leads while taying within the budget commitment of $50,000 for the campaign.

There are two types of performance goals: "results" (or "outcome") and "process" goals. Results goals focus on the specific outcome that defines success. The sales rep example above is a straightforward example of a results goal. A process goal focuses on intermediate steps that can support a broader result or outcome. So, using the same sales rep as an example, that individual could also have a process goal of "make at least thirty sales calls with potential customers per week."

Development goals

The last category of goals focuses on the employee's professional growth and development. Unfortunately, many managers neglect to include concrete development objectives when engaging in goal setting with employees. But development goals are just as critical as performance goals. All of us have skills and capabilities we need to be building to get better in our current roles, as well as to position us to take on new roles and responsibilities. Examples of development goals include:

Role	Development Goal
Sales Rep	Build confidence/capability in presenting to customers by completing 10 mock customer presentations to manager/teammates by mid-year performance review.
Engineer	Complete Design for Six Sigma certification course by end of year to advance technical capabilities and support promotion into next level.
Marketer	Build written communication skill by successfully completing online course "Writing for Creatives and Marketers" by end of Q2.

It's often the case that the presence of certain well-developed soft skills becomes the difference between the employee who moves up in the organization and the employee who is held back. If we aren't clear about development goals, we risk uneven professional development of our employees. If we do focus on them, we tend to see more motivated employees with higher morale, because they see the process as tangible evidence that you and the organization care about their learning and development.

Expectations versus goals

There is a fourth category to address as a manager, but they aren't goals per se. While goals tend to focus on *what* you want your employees to accomplish, it's also important to establish clear expectations about *how* you want your employees to go about this.

Do you expect employees to show up by 8:30 a.m. every day or are you fine if they come and go as they please as long as they accomplish their goals? Do you need them to respond to customer emails within 24 hours? Do you want them to check in with you on a daily basis or only when they need you?

In other words, are there specific behaviors you want to see them avoid or behaviors you want to see them model if they are to be successful on your team? Are there attitudes that you want to encourage or discourage? It's important to communicate these standards to teammates. The clearer you are in communicating your expectations, the better you will be at driving the behaviors, attitudes, and actions that support success on your team.

Now that we have established the importance of well-defined goals and expectations as the foundation for driving success among your team, let's look at what makes a set of goals well-defined. In this section, we'll explore best practices in goal setting.

SMART goals

No discussion on goal setting would be complete without the "SMART" goal framework. A SMART goal is:

- *Specific* — The goal must be well-defined and clear to anyone reading it such that there isn't any ambiguity.
- *Measurable* — A good goal has an objective or quantifiable way to measure whether or not it has been achieved.
- *Attainable* — The goal should stretch a person to perform at their best, but it needs to be achievable. It's a balancing act of pushing someone just out of their comfort zone, but knowing that on the whole they will have more success than failure.
- *Relevant* — The goal needs to align with the broader objectives of the team and organization to have proper impact.
- *Time-bound* — The goal needs to articulate a specific deadline by which it will be accomplished.

Weak Goal	SMART Alternative
Successfully launch new product X	Because sales of its replacement have been declining 10% per year, launch new product X by June and achieve $2M in revenue by end of year.
Become a better presenter	Attend company's presentation skills training workshop, complete three public presentations by March, and obtain manager's feedback to improve my presentation skills and position me to lead training workshops for sales reps.
Generate greater number of qualified leads than last year	Drive 10% improvement in lead generation in Q3 versus prior year through content marketing campaign in alignment with company objective of growing sales through digital marketing.

Because the SMART framework has been around for so long, countless alternative criteria have been proposed (e.g., A for action-oriented, R for realistic, among many others). The variations aren't important; the spirit of all of them is the same. If you want a particular goal to be effective, you want it to be clear, understandable, important to the bigger picture, and something that you can check back in on and establish if it's been achieved within the desired time frame without any room for debate. And if you're striking the right balance, it's also within reach, but it serves to stretch and motivate.

It's worth mentioning that, although you want to push yourself and your team to make sure goals contain these elements, there will be goals that don't lend themselves to having measurable outcomes.

For example, suppose one of your teammate's performance goals pertains to their successfully creating a high-quality slide presentation and presenting it in a big meeting. How will you measure quality when it is inherently subjective? This is a common situation that arises when setting goals. The best thing you can do is be as specific as possible about your definition of success, even if it's in qualitative terms.

By way of example, you might agree on a set of criteria you will use to gauge success such as the quality of the presentation's storyline, the accuracy of the analyses, the engagement level of the meeting participants, the success in driving the group to a decision, and so forth.

Another common challenge people face has to do with how to address any inherent arbitrariness in a given goal. Perhaps there isn't a clear external reason for when a project needs to be completed by, or maybe you're establishing a goal for year-over-year improvement on a metric and there isn't an external guideline or benchmark dictating where you should set the goal.

Even if it feels arbitrary, it's still best to establish a target because it makes the goal concrete. You can always adjust the target later to make it more appropriate. The most important thing is that you work together with your teammate to co-create the target. Sometimes that process can feel a bit like a negotiation, where they propose a number and you push them to stretch a bit further. But it's important that you land on a target for which they feel a sense of ownership and buy-in.

Remember that the SMART framework is just a guideline. Goal setting is both an art and a science, and if you're doing things well, you will be adjusting your approach to make it appropriate for the situation.

The right mix

When working with an employee to define a set of goals, experience has shown that the best mix of goals includes both performance and development goals, as well as both results and process goals.

Performance goals are critical for ensuring an employee is successful at their job and delivering on what the team and the broader organization needs from them. Development goals are essential to helping the employee level up in their skills and competencies and are strongly linked to employee engagement and retention.

Results goals are important because they clearly articulate the specific outcome an employee is trying to achieve. But it is common for the outcome embedded in a results goal to depend on factors beyond an employee's control (e.g., a product manager may have the goal of growing their category by 10 percent year over year, but other functions directly support or inhibit their ability to reach that goal).

On the other hand, process goals can be more narrowly defined such that they are under the control of an individual. This makes them a useful tool to balance with results goals. The important thing to focus on with a process goal is ensuring there is a direct cause-and-effect relationship between the process goal and the specific outcomes one is trying to achieve (e.g., in the sales rep example above, making more sales calls is a very clear productivity driver that translates into higher revenue).

The right number

One of the most common mistake managers make is pushing for (or allowing) an employee to have too many goals. These managers fall into the trap of thinking everything is important and they try to include it all. This is just another form of unrealistic goal setting. What usually happens is that the employee only has room to truly focus on a few things at a time anyway. Too many goals can cause someone who actually did a great job to feel demoralized because of their failure to accomplish every one of their goals.

Remember that there is power in focus. It's better to dig a few deep wells than to dig a dozen wells one foot deep. One of your most essential roles as a manager is to be very clear on priorities. Having clarity on what is most important and ensuring you and your team deliver on the essential will set you apart as a manager.

One rule of thumb is to aim for three primary goals, and don't exceed five. I have rarely ever exceeded three when helping my team members set up goals. In some cases, a goal may be broad, and it may need to be supported by sub-goals. As an example, you may have a primary results goal (e.g., "Deliver 10 percent efficiency improvement") and break it down into a number of process goals (e.g., "Complete time study by end of Q1"). Alternatively, you may have a primary goal over a longer time frame (e.g., "Double sales by end of year") that can be broken down into shorter-term goals (e.g., "exceed $100,000 in sales in Q1").

Once you've established a focused set of goals, be sure you and the employee agree on the relative priority level of each of the performance goals. One way to do this is to assign a percentage weight correlating with the importance level or the expected time/effort spent across the goals. This keeps everyone honest. It also may lead you to the recognition that it would be better to remove certain goals from the list (e.g., if 80 percent of employee effort is geared toward the top goal and 5 percent is left for the bottom goal, it probably makes sense to cut the bottom goal).

The right time frame

The pace of change in organizations has increased in recent decades, and there is no sign of it slowing. Many companies and organizations of all types have been faced with the need to change their dated performance management systems to align with the speed of modern times. It's naïve to think that an employee can set a goal in the beginning of the year and have that goal remain relevant throughout the entirety of the year. Things come up. Conditions change. Priorities need to be revised.

While the right time frame for goal setting will vary based on the particular role and situation, it's best to think about goals as cascading, where annual goals are composed of semi-annual or quarterly goals, and those are broken down further if appropriate.

Through experience, I have landed on quarterly goal setting as being the most broadly useful time frame to focus on for most roles and situations. It allows sufficient time to drive meaningful results, but it is a short enough time window to allow for the frequent adjustments that need to be made as priorities shift throughout the year. It also enables you to address shortfalls and performance issues that arise along the way in a timely fashion. Goals don't always change quarter to quarter, and sometimes they only require small refinements (such as revising what turned out to be an unrealistic goal to make it more achievable). But reviewing goals every quarter encourages accountability and it supports your efforts to manage up in an effective way—a topic we will delve into in more depth in a later chapter.

A final word about goals and expectations

One of the characteristics we see in superb leaders is that they have clarity about where they want to go in the form of a vision and strategy, they consistently socialize it within and beyond their teams, they have an achievable plan for how to get there, and they demonstrate their ability to deliver on expectations by executing against that plan. And what is successful execution of a plan but a case of setting and achieving goals?

Goal setting is a big topic and it's one you see many leaders struggle to get right. But if you're working with your team to write out goals according to the principles we have just discussed, and if you take the time to frequently revisit and adjust those goals, you will gain the benefits of effective goal setting even if some of the goals turn out not to have been perfectly defined on your first attempt.

Time and again, when dissecting the drivers of success of leading organizations, you find highly effective goal setting from top to bottom in that organization. It's for this reason that I encourage you to spend the time to master the art and science of goal setting if you want to reach your full potential as a great manager.

Chapter 4:

Prioritization, Delegation,

and Time Management

Now that you've established clear goals, you can be confident you and your team members are aiming at the right targets. But there are many potential routes from where you and your team are today to where you want to be. As a manager, your next major responsibility is to guide your team through the iterative work-planning and execution process that optimizes your team's route from point A to point B.

The specific approach you use is going to depend on your particular area of responsibility. Success in some roles requires having detailed roadmaps and project plans that lay out every step of the process, in complete granularity, that you and your team need to execute. Other roles are inherently more fluid and do not lend themselves to such a systematic approach.

Regardless, the thought process is the same. You need to break your team's bigger-picture goals down into digestible work streams, prioritize which of those are the most important, ensure the work is divided among your team in an optimal way through effective delegation, and employ effective time management techniques as you guide ongoing execution.

Prioritization

One of the most common sources of negative feedback in employee surveys about their direct managers as well as upper management is: "There aren't clear priorities." This feedback can also show up in association with other verbiage, such as "Management lacks a vision/strategy" or "Management lacks focus." If you dig a level deeper underneath this feedback, you find a range of potential underlying issues. Here are the most common:

1. Priorities have not been defined.
2. Priorities have been defined, but they have not been communicated effectively.
3. There are too many priorities.
4. Priorities change too frequently.

The reason prioritization is one the most common complaints in employee surveys is because it isn't a skill most people have honed. That's even true of a big portion of the people who land in CEO and top leadership roles. All too often, leaders succumb to the temptation of trying to take on too much. Likewise, leaders often fall prey to "shiny penny syndrome," where they become too prone to shifting their attention from existing priorities in order to chase new opportunities that pop up.

This is where critical thinking comes into play. There is a reason critical thinking is consistently rated as one of the most essential characteristics of outstanding leaders. It is the leader's job to ensure that an organization is executing on the right priorities and to guard against the many forces that distract attention or dilute organizational focus. It is the leader's job to discern signal from noise. It is the leader's job to be strategic, to know when to say "no," and to have the discipline to follow through with that.

To be a top manager, you need to constantly exercise your critical thinking capability, taking a step back and asking yourself questions such as, "Are we still aiming in the right direction? Has anything vital changed since we established these priorities? Do our current priorities still reflect the most important things for us to execute on? Does our execution to date suggest we need to make any adjustments to our priorities?"

It's from this bigger view that you should always be aware of what work streams and tasks are on your critical path and ensure that those, above all else, are resourced appropriately.

Likewise, it's from this bigger view that you should always be looking for how the Pareto principle may pertain to your priority list and use that to further focus your efforts on the most important things. (The Pareto principle, also referred to as the "80/20 rule," states that in general, 80 percent of the effects come from 20 percent of the causes.) Our first instinct as managers is often to spread our team's efforts as though we're hedging our bets, when often we would be better off doubling down our efforts on a couple of high-priority items and ensuring we knock those out of the park.

At the specialty vehicle manufacturer, Oshkosh, the company lives by the 80/20 rule and uses it to drive focus in everything they do. They consistently reemphasize the need for what they call "80/20 focus" in meetings, and they push their organization to clearly state the priority (or to clearly state any shift in priority) that results from any discussion they have. Furthermore, every resulting priority is well-defined within the context of each individual's role, which enables that person to successfully execute on the priority.

It is a good standard practice to consistently reiterate priorities to your team. Rather than it being a one-time discussion, revisiting priorities in discussions and pushing everyone to look at them through the 80/20 lens helps to surface any issues or areas of misalignment quickly, and it ensures the team's big-picture priorities are optimized. A strong manager continually asks questions to trigger that discussion and teaches their team to think that way.

But top managers don't just operate at the big-picture level, they also need to be able to drill down multiple levels into details, to gauge progress at that level, and to make adjustments as necessary. The best managers consistently oscillate between the big picture and the granular, checking in to ensure things are on course at the strategic level (and making adjustments as needed), then diving back down to a more granular level to ensure execution is progressing (and making adjustments at that level as needed).

The world's best managers are ruthlessly focused on prioritization. But remember, it's not enough to have a set of clear priorities in your head or written down somewhere. It's not even enough to have a set of clear priorities that you've clearly communicated to all of the appropriate stakeholders. The way prioritization becomes real is through resource allocation. Your actual priorities are reflected through who you have assigned to each priority, how much of their effort/time is allocated to that priority, and the degree to which that priority is supported by any other requirements (e.g., funding, support from other functions, etc.).

Delegation

Delegation of work stems from the priorities you set.

Effective delegation is one of the areas new managers struggle most to learn. Every so often, a new manager will come along and be over-the-top with respect to delegation because they're on a power trip resulting from their new position of authority. But by far the more common difficulty new managers have is the tendency not to delegate enough to their teammates.

Why?

Sometimes a new manager has trouble letting go of doing the work, especially if they perceive the quality of the work produced by those reporting to them as being less than what they themselves could produce. This is a common trap for new managers and can result in micromanagement. This happens when the new manager does not trust the team sufficiently and does not yet grasp that everything does not have to be done his or her way—that there are many ways to "skin the cat." Your team's work may not be perfectly aligned with what you wanted, but ask yourself the question, "Is it good enough, or perhaps even better than what I had in mind?" Many times, the answer to that is "yes," and you can start to let go of the reins and focus more on providing good guidance.

As a consultant, one of my best-performing team members had just transitioned to the manager role and it was his first time leading a project—in this case for large pool chemical manufacturer. I observed that he spent about 20 percent extra time on that project because he wanted the outcome to be perfect and was doing almost everything himself to achieve this "perfection." However, after several weeks of taking this approach, we sat down and discussed the long hours he was working. The major driver of his unsustainable schedule was his reluctance to delegate because he was not sure his team members were capable of delivering to my expectations. I shared with him that it is better to let them try and coach them first and only step in and take over a work stream as a last resort. A few weeks later, I saw his hours going down because he finally embraced delegating, teaching, and empowering his team. From then on, he discovered he had more leverage than ever and was able to accomplish things as a team he never would have been able to accomplish as a one-man show.

Often, managers need to train one of their team members on a task if they hope to offload that work. Because it takes more time to teach someone how to do something compared with just doing it themselves, and because they tend to feel time-crunched and under a lot of pressure to perform in their new role, new managers sometimes default to doing the task themselves.

It also takes some people time to get used to asking other people to do things for them. This is a common feeling among new managers, and it naturally leads to many managers avoiding asking for support from their team in certain cases. But, as long as one is delegating in a respectful and appropriate way, there is no need to feel this way.

Despite all of these reasons that can hold a new manager back from delegating, sooner or later you learn that effective delegation equals survival. You can't possibly be everywhere. You can't possibly do everything. And most of the time, you can't even oversee every single work product, at least not to the level you might want to review it. There isn't enough time. If there is enough time to do that, then chances are you might be in a position where you are being under-utilized, which is not a great place to be.

Delegate, delegate, delegate.

It's not just for your benefit, either. Your team members need to be given the right tasks and projects to ensure they are satisfied in their roles and that their professional development is progressing.

So, delegate.

There are several decisions you are implicitly making when you delegate a task. First, you are deciding if it's a task that you should do or one that somebody else should do. If it's the latter, then you may also be deciding which person on your team is the appropriate person to take it on (unless that's clear based on how the task fits in with previously defined roles and responsibilities). You're also deciding how close you need to stay to the work—some things are so critical that they require substantial involvement from you, whereas other things may not be a good use of your time. And lastly, you are implicitly deciding if a task is necessary. (Remember that you should always be revisiting things and looking for opportunities to streamline and eliminate non-essential tasks.)

The Eisenhower decision matrix is a framework that can be used to guide some of this thought process:

	Non-Urgent	Urgent
Important to Project Objectives	Important activities, but can be led by the team with your direction **"You can delegate the underlying work** because there is time, but need to stay closely involved"	Important activities that require higher level attention to the work and sense of urgency **"You do the work** with support from the team"
Less important to Project Objectives	Activities that are slow burn and can often be eliminated "You have a discussion with the team/client on whether these things are really needed or **can be eliminated**"	Activities that do not require the highest perfection or insight, but have a sense of urgency **"Delegate** these activities where possible, **give adequate attention** to the ones you can't delegate to avoid negative repercussions"

One of the valuable things about the decision matrix is that it highlights one of the more difficult things to discern in your day-to-day work—the difference between the Urgent and the Important. Urgent items tend to take over most people's focus because of time sensitivity, often crowding out the less urgent yet vitally important tasks in the process.

A skilled manager uses delegation as a tool to ensure that they themselves are spending as much time as possible focused on the most important things and those that can only be done by them.

It's rare that managers have a problem prioritizing their time correctly on the Important/Urgent tasks. The challenge arises with getting swallowed up by Less-Important/Urgent tasks, and not spending enough time on the Important/Non-Urgent items.

The first place a manager should start is with ruthless focus and elimination of any truly unnecessary tasks in the Less-Important/Non-Urgent category. A lot of our "nice-to-haves" fall in this category. It once took me six months before I realized reorganizing our team's file-sharing database needed to be pulled off our team task list. It would have been satisfying, but the incremental time-saving from a more intuitive file hierarchy wasn't worth it. That was a lesson in needing to be more ruthless in the focus I applied to my team's time.

The next thing a manager should always do is to look at the remaining task list and ask, "What can I delegate?"

It's especially critical to delegate as many of the Less-Important/Urgent tasks to make room for time to focus on the Important tasks (both Urgent and Non-Urgent) that only you can do. As an example, when I was in charge of product development, I would receive many calls to attend another function's quarterly meetings to present our product plan. These were time-sensitive and needed to happen, but I didn't always need to be the person attending the meetings. So these became tasks I delegated, which freed me up and gave my teammates both an opportunity to practice presenting and exposure to the wider organization.

Delegation is the place to start, but there will be Less-Important/Urgent tasks you simply can't delegate. Those tasks still require your attention; left undone, they will have a negative impact over time. For example, if you push off doing your expense report long enough, eventually it goes from a Non-Urgent to an Urgent task. Unless you have administrative support, you just need to get it done. We all have lots of these types of tasks. Do your best to give them the appropriate level of attention without having too much of your time swallowed up by Less-Important/Urgent items.

The other place to pay particular attention to is delegating an appropriate level of Important/Urgent and Important/Non-Urgent work. Because of the importance level, you'll still need to remain involved and provide guidance throughout the execution of these tasks. But there are almost always portions of the work that can be appropriately delegated to free you up to play your managerial role.

I use the Eisenhower matrix at the beginning of every day to look at what is on my to-do list, and for each task, I prioritize it for myself, I delegate it, or I push it out (or eliminate it entirely). At first, you might need to actually write down your to-dos in the four boxes, but this will become natural through routine. I promise that if you adopt this routine, it will show through to the people on your team. The result is that they will view you as more on-point and clear about team priorities, and they will also see you as a more effective delegator.

When there is a choice as to whom on your team to delegate a task, there are many factors that can impact your decision. We won't go into all of the possible factors, but we will look at two particularly useful frames to keep in mind.

The first frame to remember is that your job as a leader is to drive the performance of the organization (financial or otherwise, depending on the nature of the organization) through optimal allocation of resources. The relative value/cost of people's time is not equal simply on the basis of how much money they are paid by the organization. As an example, it wouldn't make sense to use your most "expensive" asset (which could be your senior-most team member, or it could be you) to execute a simple, repetitive, time-consuming task that could be effectively delegated to a more junior employee.

This may seem obvious, but it's a more common mistake than you would expect. Don't be surprised if someday you find yourself saying, "Oh, I'll just do this myself," because the rest of your team is fully loaded, and you see that as the path of least resistance. Or you may find you're giving a task to someone simply because they have more bandwidth, when it would be more appropriate to give that task to somebody else and rebalance workloads accordingly.

So, use your team resources wisely, and that includes your own time.

All of this needs to be balanced by the second frame — the needs and capabilities of your team. You wouldn't want to load your lowest-level employee with only grunt work or they won't grow and develop, and you might soon find that you have an opening to fill because they've decided they've had enough. Or a project could come along that is the perfect growth opportunity for one of your team members, even though on the surface it might appear to be a stretch for them and a slam dunk for another team member. Alternatively, a critically important task could come along that is in the sweet spot of one of your "A Players," and you may determine you cannot risk delegating it to anyone but that team member.

In the end, every decision you make—from completely hands-off delegation to delegating with lots of coaching and oversight—needs to pass one litmus test without fail: you have to have the appropriate level of bandwidth to fulfill your end of the bargain as the manager on the scene. So, do your best to keep track of your own workload and consider your level of involvement carefully in delegation decisions.

When it comes to the act of delegating itself, it's simple as long as you remember to follow a few easy rules.

First, be respectful when you delegate. This can be done by asking somebody to take on a task in a kind tone, often in the form of a question. For example, "Joe, will you review this presentation and add citations everywhere we've included data or a graph?"

Second, make sure you're specific about the time frame within which you need something completed, and that you spell out any other process-oriented requests. This is the time to be clear about your level of involvement and any other expectations you have. Building on our previous example, you might say "Joe, will you add citations throughout this presentation and send it to Suzie by Friday at noon? I don't need to review it." Or "Joe, will you take a first pass at adding citations to this presentation by Wednesday morning so we can get together that afternoon and discuss them? After that, if you will finalize and send to me by Friday morning, I can then email it to Suzie by Friday at noon when she needs it."

Often this is the point at which things would naturally turn into a discussion, since you and Joe may need to go back and forth about his availability, bandwidth, and any priorities that need to be rebalanced as a result of this new request. The mere act of discussing what a team member has on their plate and how the incoming task results in rebalancing priorities will set you apart from most managers and it will build loyalty among your team. Too many managers leave interactions like this with their employees feeling like their manager has no concept of how much they're being asked to do, or that their manager has little respect for their time.

Third, ask your team member if the request is clear enough and see if they have follow-up questions in that moment. It's common for us to think that the request we've communicated is clear, but there are lots of reasons why the task may not be defined effectively enough for the employee to run with it yet.

Fourth, reiterate that they should come find you at any point along the way if they have any questions pop up, and thank them in advance for their support. By demonstrating your availability and willingness to engage, you are showing them that the task is important to you and that you value them for the help they are providing.

Time management

As a manager, you are coordinating a lot of activity across a number of people. On any given day, you may be checking in with various teammates on a variety of work streams, pushing forward on the work that only you can do, revisiting priorities, managing up, communicating with colleagues in other groups, and any number of other things, not to mention fighting fires.

In fact, based on my work with many hundreds of managers at all levels of organizations, it's best to assume that one-third of your day will be spent dealing with things you didn't expect to have on your plate when you woke up that morning. Most days, you won't feel like you have one-third of a day to divert. But you'll have to work through it nonetheless.

Make sure you understand where you can flex scheduled time daily because you will always have to.

At times, this may feel exhilarating. You are a key player at the nexus of important things that need to come together, and people are depending on you.

At other times, this can feel chaotic and stressful.

While there is no way to avoid having to face chaotic times, the best way to position yourself so that you're able to navigate all of the competing demands on your and your team's time is to employ good time management practices.

One of the most powerful stories I have to share regarding the importance of discipline with respect to priorities and time management came during my time working with an agriculture company. An older gentleman I had periodically engaged with over the course of my project work was a farmer in Iowa. At one point, I reached out to him to see if I could meet with him for an hour. He responded politely, but powerfully, that our meeting would have to wait until after the harvest season was over because he only gets thirty harvests in his entire life to make a living and generate enough wealth to support his family.

This struck me hard because I saw how this same idea applies to so many situations in my own life.

You only have so many opportunities to get in front of certain people and make an impression. You only have so many truly critical meetings and milestones that are capable of altering the trajectory of your career. You only have so many morning coffee meetups with coworkers.

How would you approach certain situations if you knew they numbered in the single digits?

When you boil it down, time management is about the discipline of giving attention where attention is due. It is the discipline to focus the bulk of your time and effort on that which is most essential. It can be difficult to keep track of everything, but when you lose track, that's when you get mismatches between the priority level of something and the time and effort you and your team put toward it.

This is where systems come into play. The better you are able to systematize aspects of your team's execution of day-to-day tasks, the less likely things are to fall through the cracks or become imbalanced. There are many tools available to support you in managing your and your team's time. Tools like Slack, Microsoft Teams, TaskRay, and Trello are designed to support you in project management, collaboration, and time management. It's likely your organization has a subscription to a service like this or is willing to have you subscribe if they do not. Take time to define and hone your and your team's work processes and employ such tools where helpful.

Time management isn't just about optimizing execution and ensuring you achieve your goals. It is also critical for ensuring you and your team achieve work/life balance and avoid burnout. Mark Schwabero, the retired CEO of Brunswick Corporation, put this way: "Everybody is juggling a lot of balls in the air, both personally and professionally. It's important to know which ones are rubber and will bounce when dropped, and which are glass."

Everyone juggles a lot of balls, but it is important to distinguish the rubber balls from the glass balls to avoid critical failures.

This is language I have used with my own team with respect to time management. During meetings, we take time to discuss whether there are any "glass balls" on any of our projects that we need to address differently to ensure we don't drop them. But we also use the language with respect to personal priorities. If somebody tells me they have something going on at home that is a "glass ball," then they are free to leave so they can be there for that, no questions asked. Respecting people's time and their personal priorities is one of the most vital ways to build a loyal and cohesive team.

The world's best managers do not need to resort to burning their teams out. Yet it's becoming increasingly common for managers to do just that. Don't be one of those managers. Be one of the great ones. You can achieve results and do so in an inspiring way. People will follow you as a result.

There is so much more to say on time management than could be fit into this book. Not only that, but we could fill libraries with the plethora of books that have already been written on time management over the years. So, if time management is an area you could brush up on, seek out one of the many fine resources that speaks to you. It will be time well spent. Good time management is vital for accomplishing your goals and doing so in a way that promotes a healthy work environment for you and your team.

Chapter 5:

Coaching, Feedback, and Writing Reviews

When introducing you to the essential characteristics of top-tier managers, we ended with a key point—that great managers are teachers. In fact, no matter what research you look to or which surveys you reference, you almost always find this common theme: superior managers focus as much effort on coaching and developing the individuals on their team as they do on setting strategy and guiding execution. They know this will pay dividends, because their results are only as good as the team they have supporting them—and the quality of their team is dramatically influenced by the degree to which they coach and develop those individuals.

Fundamentally, this boils down to an attitude of placing the welfare and development of your team members above everything else. Great managers put the team first. Great managers care about the individuals they are responsible for managing. Great managers want to see their employees succeed. Great managers help their team members learn and grow. Great managers listen. Great managers empower team members to make decisions and offer support and guidance to help course correct along the way. Yes, at times a manager needs to be directive and decisive, but the best managers are always looking for opportunities to boost their team members and empower them.

But it's about more than just having this attitude. To do all of this well, it must be backed up by an essential competency: providing feedback in an effective way. Feedback is the primary means by which you help guide an employee up the learning curve on all of the various aspects of their professional development.

UCLA basketball coach John Wooden once said, "A good coach can give correction without causing resentment." This points to the essence of why there is an art and science to giving feedback. If you don't give feedback in the right way, it may lead to negative reactions like defensiveness or even resentment. And there is no way to damage a working relationship and your collective productivity faster than by triggering resentment or other forms of negativity in a team member.

This risk, however, should not deter a manager from giving consistent feedback. Frequent feedback is essential to a strong manager/employee relationship that is rooted in learning and development.

In this section, we are going to dive into the nuances of delivering feedback in the optimal way. Giving feedback takes quite a bit of practice, so if you're new to management, it may not come naturally during your early attempts. But you will get better with repetition.

It's also natural for you to feel uncomfortable or anxious early on when it comes to giving feedback. Even a seasoned manager may experience those feelings before a particularly difficult or sensitive feedback discussion. With time and practice, most of those feelings subside and you will find that you can approach even difficult situations with poise and confidence.

When it comes to giving feedback, there are two primary types: ongoing feedback and formal feedback. We will explore both of these in more depth in a moment. But before doing that, let's cover some principles that apply regardless of the type of feedback you're giving.

Make it a dialog

In any feedback interaction, it should always be a two-way exchange as opposed to a one-way lecture. You want your team member to ask follow-up questions if they have any.

In a case where they are open to the feedback or they agree with the point you are conveying, discussion and follow-up questions open up greater opportunity to maximize learning in the moment.

In the case where the team member refutes or pushes back when receiving the feedback (which is usually more of an exception than the norm), it's important to understand their point of view. Perhaps you haven't seen the situation clearly. By listening to their point of view, you may find that you come away with a reshaped perspective. Even if that isn't the case, you still want your team members to feel heard and understood.

So, any way you look at it, you will get better outcomes if you make a feedback interaction a dialog. Therefore, head into such a situation prepared to invite discussion, and most of all, be prepared to listen.

Structure feedback using the SBIS framework

What are you trying to accomplish when you are communicating a piece of feedback to one of your team members?

At the most basic level, you want them to walk away from that interaction and actually implement changes to how they operate in some way, or you want them to keep doing something they're doing well and provide encouragement. Simultaneously, you want them to come away from the interaction feeling as good as possible about it given the nature of the feedback. (In most cases, you want your team member feeling good, but there will be tougher discussions where it would be unrealistic to expect them to walk away "feeling good." Even in such cases, you want the employee to feel like the discussion was fair and respectful.) Those two qualities constitute the essence of success when discussing a piece of feedback.

Of course, on top of that you may be trying to accomplish other goals, such as wanting that team member to feel supported and motivated, or wanting them to know how invested you are in their professional development. But fundamentally, you've succeeded in an interaction if the team member can reliably use that discussion to hone how they do their job, and they come away feeling reasonably good about the interaction.

For feedback to check those two important boxes in a consistent way, it needs to include several elements without fail.

First and foremost, it's essential that feedback be grounded in a specific, real-world example (or multiple examples). When you provide feedback, the individual needs to be clear on what they did well or what they could have done better, the rationale for why that is the case, and how they should go about things when faced with a similar situation in the future. A real-world example makes all of this concrete by giving them much needed context and color.

The opposite of doing this is delivering general, vague, or abstract feedback (e.g., "You have good poise." "You aren't forceful enough.") General feedback that is not paired with concrete examples is difficult for people to act on. Often, the very reason a person continues to act in a certain way is because it is natural and automatic for them. Their behavior or action may even be unconscious to them, so hearing about it in general language may not be enough for them to recognize what you are trying to point out. By contextualizing it with an example, you help make it real and increase the chances the person is able to recognize it and act on it as well.

Beyond these benefits, real-world examples are also important for the occasional situation you encounter where somebody reacts with defensiveness. While you should never treat the real-world examples as though they are evidence in a case you are arguing like a prosecuting attorney—that's a surefire way to cause somebody to close off to the feedback—having examples can be the difference between that person continuing to resist versus having them open their mind to the point of view you are sharing.

Because they are such a critical ingredient, I want to share two ways to help ensure you always have solid examples to support a piece of feedback you are delivering.

Here's the first way: When you observe something you want to help reinforce or correct, share feedback as soon as you can after the observation. That doesn't mean you should share it right in that moment. Usually you shouldn't. (We will talk more about the appropriate time and environment to deliver feedback shortly.) But the longer you wait, the more the memory of the situation is likely to fade (for both of you), and the less timely and relevant the feedback is to the employee.

The second method is a simple hack I've recommended to many managers throughout the years: When an example arises that supports a future feedback discussion, take a few seconds to capture it somewhere. Some people will write it down. Some people send a quick email to themselves and drop the email into a specific folder focused on their team's professional development. Others create a space in a notes app and jot it down in there. When you adopt one of these approaches, you have a place you know you can go to refresh your memory on specific examples before going into feedback sessions or writing performance reviews. Examples pop up at random times and fade from your memory just as quickly. Create a system that works for you to capture and document them so that you don't lose track of this important raw material for professional development conversations.

As you can tell by how much time I have devoted to this topic, grounding feedback in specific examples is tremendously important. That alone is more than half the battle when it comes to having an effective feedback discussion. But there are other key elements every piece of feedback needs to reflect, so let's explore those now.

The next essential aspect to feedback is that it needs to rise to the level of importance to be worthy of discussion in the first place. There is little value in discussing trivial points of feedback. The desirable or undesirable behaviors or actions warrant discussion if they have a material impact on the success of the team or if they pertain to development areas that an individual needs to focus on to grow and expand professionally. For that reason, it's ideal if you can link the piece of feedback to performance criteria that are part of that team member's development plan or that are a part of your team or organization's performance review process.

It may seem like an obvious point that you should only share feedback that reaches a certain threshold of importance, but if you've ever had a manager who corrects every little behavior they spot that isn't to their liking, you understand why it's worth mentioning. Nobody wants to work for those managers.

If you spot a sub-optimal behavior for the first time, it's often best to wait and see if your team member corrects it on their own the next time. Often people do, and it's frustrating for anyone to have every little mistake pointed out, including the ones they were aware that they made in the moment.

But once you have reason to suspect something is a pattern, then it is appropriate to have a discussion about it.

There are two main exceptions to this guidance. First, if it's important that the behavior not be repeated because of potentially meaningful consequences, nip it in the bud. Second, you don't need to wait if you are early on in a working relationship and there is a mutual understanding that you are in a hands-on and corrective mode of management for a period of time.

The last crucial element to feedback is that it needs to be highly actionable. This means that the team member can walk away and immediately know what to do when faced with a similar situation in the future.

Grounding feedback in a real-world example helps provide the contextual understanding that makes something actionable. Sharing the positive or negative consequence the behavior had and linking it to performance or development criteria provides the person the impetus to take action.

The final ingredient is the *how*. Here, you will want to be prepared to solicit potential solutions from the individual. How can they hone their actions in the future? It's always best to invite potential solutions from the employee first. But having a recommendation in your back pocket is a good idea in case they struggle to identify a possible solution themselves.

To ensure you are delivering a piece of feedback in a way that accomplishes all of these various objectives — that it's grounded in a real example, that it's focused on a behavior or action of meaningful consequence, and that it can be effectively acted upon — I strongly urge you to follow the structure below. This framework will help to ensure that your feedback interaction includes every one of the essential elements we have discussed.

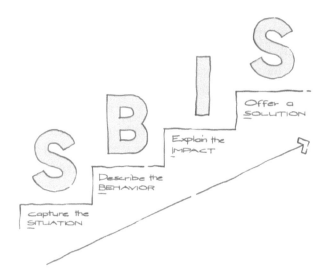

The SBIS Framework: Situation, Behavior, Impact, Solution

Capturing the situation and describing the behavior is the means by which you ground the feedback in a real-world example. Explaining the impact demonstrates that the feedback is meaningful and important enough to rise to a level of needing to discuss it. It also provides the impetus for change (or for continuing a positive behavior). Asking questions ensures you are having a dialog and allows your teammate to be heard. It also gives you the opportunity to pivot if you have misread a situation. Inviting a solution teaches teammates to solve their own issues, places their professional development in their own hands, and ensures the feedback becomes actionable.

One of the most powerful effects of using the SBIS framework is that it removes *you* from the feedback situation. If a piece of feedback feels to an employee like it stems only from your opinions, your peers and employees are less likely to accept it and are more likely to take it personally. But presented through the SBIS framework, you become the messenger of an objective observation supported by facts. This is the key to helping ensure that person receives the feedback well.

This framework was especially helpful for me when I was first transitioning to becoming a manager and had to give some very tough feedback to an underperforming employee who was misinterpreting nearly everything our client was saying. This employee was a very proud person, older than me, and the first few times I gave him feedback, he snapped at me because I fumbled the message or sandwiched the feedback. Once I learned about the SBIS framework and used it to explain to him how his actions were impacting our success on the project, he understood, embraced the feedback, and internalized the change.

Below are two examples of effectively delivering a piece of feedback using the SBIS framework:

Positive/reinforcing feedback using SBIS framework:

1.   Capture the Situation

"Emma, during the service call you had with the customer this morning, you had to manage a very charged situation."

2. Describe the Behavior

"As the customer escalated the situation, you kept an even tone, you showed no visible signs of frustration, and you were calm as you worked toward a solution."

3. Explain the Impact and Ask Questions
"This de-escalated a situation that could have threatened our business with this important customer. Does that make sense?"

4. Invite Potential Solutions
"Is there anything I can do to continue supporting you as a manager to help you keep up this good work?"

Constructive feedback using SBIS framework:
1. Capture the Situation
"Marty, in the staff meeting yesterday, you had to present the results of the analyses you have been working on over the past three weeks."

2. Describe the Behavior
"Throughout the presentation, your body language conveyed low confidence. For example, you were looking at the floor as you summarized your main takeaways and your voice became very quiet as you fielded some of the more challenging questions from the team."

3. Explain the Impact and Ask Questions
"I could see that your body language and tone of voice were reducing the amount of confidence the team had in the quality of your analyses and your conclusions, even though I know the quality of the work was high from the check-ins we had. Does this make sense? Do you agree?"

4. Invite Potential Solutions
"What do you recommend you do to learn how to display more confidence through your voice and your body language?"

(If Marty struggles to come up with actionable ideas, you can then support him by offering a suggestion like this: "I'll send you a link to a TED talk video that highlights the power of body language that has some useful recommendations. Why don't you start by watching that and let's reconnect later so you can share with me ideas for how you can practice?")

One of the most important things to call attention to with the examples above is that SBIS should be used with *positive and negative feedback*. By using the framework for positive feedback, it ensures the individual understands *why* they did something well. By doing this, they will most likely strive to repeat it. Delivering feedback in this way is orders of magnitude more powerful than "Hey, great job on…." Try it and you'll see the effect. Most people haven't received positive feedback in this way. When they do, they are often stunned in a good way.

Each of the above examples sticks to the script and follows the SBIS flow from start to finish. But similar to the SMART goal framework, SBIS is just a guideline and it isn't something you have to follow one hundred percent of the time. Sometimes a small situation arises where it's more appropriate to offer a simple coaching suggestion, such as the examples that follow:

- "Vera, next time before jumping right into the content of the meeting, will you remind people what we discussed in the previous meeting? It will help ensure everyone is on the same page about where we left off and what we need to accomplish."
- "Sam, next time you run out of time and the customer tells you they have to go, remember to

thank them and let them know they can reach out to you any time with questions. The customer will feel more supported and less like they are burdening you if they do need to come back to you with questions."

- "Vera, you did a great job repeating every question in the Q&A portion of your presentation before answering the question. That helped ensure everyone heard the question and it made the questioner feel like they were truly heard as well."

- "Sam, nice work on the financial analysis you submitted. By taking the time to address all of the board's questions with the analysis, you really made it clear which project we should prioritize."

In these short examples as well as the two longer SBIS examples above, I have shared an equal proportion of positive and negative/constructive feedback.

In reality, I recommend giving six positive pieces of feedback using the framework for every negative one. This compliment-to-criticism ratio helps ensure that the person you are managing stays in a positive frame of mind and doesn't default to a defensive posture when you deliver feedback.

Remember that while SBIS is an effective way to frame how you communicate a piece of feedback to an individual, the success of any coaching interaction depends upon you fostering a two-way dialog. It's crucial that you listen to the other person to gauge their reaction and understanding, to make sure they feel heard, to ensure they are bought into the solution, to encourage them to take ownership over their own professional development, and, on occasion, to revise your feedback based on them having a different, valid perspective about the situation at hand.

There are two ways to help ensure the coaching interaction is a two-way dialog.

The first way is to ask questions. This is built into the SBIS framework after explaining the impact, but questions need not be limited to that point in the conversation. It's also good practice to ask questions that draw the person into collaboratively agreeing upon an optimal solution for the situation, as this reinforces their ownership over their professional development. Or it may be appropriate to ask questions earlier in the discussion. For example, suppose you see the person immediately becoming disengaged before you're able to convey your main points. This might be a good time to stop to ask if everything is okay or if it would be better to find a different time to have this discussion.

The other method for promoting good dialog is a simple technique I call "practicing the pause," which means that you hold back your urge to jump in and fill silence with more talking, and instead leave ample space as an invitation for the other person to think and respond. Doing this shows the other person you want to hear their point of view and that you truly are focused on listening and helping them rather than just getting your point across.

Now that we've talked about how to effectively structure a feedback conversation, we're going to dive into the two types of feedback.

Ongoing feedback

As the name suggests, ongoing feedback is the type of coaching and guidance you provide on a day-to-day basis. The frequency of this feedback will likely vary based on who the employee is and where they are in their stage of development, among other factors. Generally, more feedback is better. While it is possible to overdo it, as we discussed earlier in the example of the over-correcting manager, most people do not overdo it. Most err on the side of too little feedback. So, for that reason, "more is better" is a reasonable piece of advice for the typical manager.

That being said, what primarily dictates the frequency of ongoing feedback is the *need*. When somebody is learning a skill and you see an opportunity for them to improve, that is a trigger to deliver feedback that helps them adjust. Likewise, if somebody is learning a skill and they do something well that you have not yet acknowledged, that is a trigger to deliver feedback that reinforces the positive action.

When giving ongoing feedback, there are several things you will want to do.

First and foremost, be prepared. This can't be emphasized enough. Off-the-cuff feedback often comes across poorly and it can backfire. Take the time to gather concrete examples or assemble the examples you have already captured along the way in your professional development notes as we discussed earlier. Organize your thoughts according to the SBIS framework, making notes and talking points for yourself that you can refer to during the discussion.

Before offering feedback to somebody, ask them for their permission to do so. For example, you could use a phrase like, "May I share some observations with you?" Unless it's positive/reinforcing feedback, be sure to frame it as an opportunity for them develop as opposed to "constructive criticism." Together, these can help ease anxiety and set the stage for an open and productive conversation rather than a potential confrontation. This goes a long way toward building trust and receptivity with your team members.

Make sure your feedback is well-structured and you are hitting the key points (using the SBIS framework if appropriate for the situation), and do your best to deliver the feedback with confidence. You believe what you are saying to be true. Don't undermine it by waffling or conveying doubt through a timid tone or weak body language.

Encourage dialog through questions like, "Does that make sense?" Once you ask a question, *practice the pause* and focus on listening and gauging the individual's reaction through their words and body language. If it's clear they understand and agree with your feedback, then thank them for their time and let them know they can come to you with questions as they arise. But if you sense they don't understand or that they may disagree with the feedback, ask questions in an open, non-confrontational way to draw that out so the two of you can discuss it.

In general, the best time to give ongoing feedback is soon after you observe something that needs correcting or reinforcing, but not immediately after it happens.

If you jump all over something too quickly, a person can feel picked apart and start to become overly self-conscious.

This can cause them to be on guard. They may start to feel like you are judging them at all times and that you're ready to pounce on their mistakes at any moment. This is particularly problematic with team members who struggle with confidence. You can set them back by being feedback-heavy in this way.

On the other hand, the longer you wait, the less timely and relevant the real-world example is to the person you are giving the feedback. Also, if you wait too long, even a small piece of feedback can feel like it's been blown out of proportion (e.g., "Was it really a big enough deal that you're still thinking about it four weeks later?"). And waiting too long can contribute to people feeling like you're keeping score. (One exception to this concern about waiting too long is when you go back to older examples during a formal performance review. But the performance review shouldn't be the first time you're sharing the older examples with them.)

So how long should you wait? It's generally best if you discuss it later that day, the next day, or the next appropriate opportunity that arises that week. That strikes the right balance of having it feel organic and keeping it timely and fresh, but not overdoing it and having people see you as an overly critical judge.

The other thing waiting just a little while allows for is selecting the right time and forum to deliver feedback. Except on the rarest of occasions, it is almost *never* appropriate to give negative feedback to an individual in front of other people. Feedback should be a private conversation. Not only that, but you want to catch the person in the right frame of mind. If you can tell they are stressed and flustered, wait until they are likely to be in a more receptive mood.

As for location, it's great if it can be in person because it conveys the importance you place on their professional development and it allows you to read their body language. But for ongoing feedback, phone is a fine alternative in most situations, particularly if it means you can deliver feedback in a timelier fashion than you could if you waited until the next in-person opportunity arose.

The last point to make with ongoing feedback is to reinforce the message of providing the right balance of positive/reinforcing and constructive feedback. Don't mistake this for the old concept of the "positive sandwich," where you sandwich something negative or constructive between two positive things. Don't do that. You may think it makes the feedback more palatable, but it waters down the message and it is far less effective. When delivering a piece of feedback, think of it as one single point you want to make and stay consistent with the SBIS framework. Providing balance between types of feedback means that if the last piece of feedback you gave to your team member was constructive, it's time to provide five or six points of positive/reinforcing feedback to help encourage and motivate them.

If you're able to assimilate what we have discussed into your approach for giving ongoing feedback, the process will start to feel organic and natural. When something comes up, you'll address it expeditiously. Feedback won't feel charged or loaded, it's just one flavor of conversation you have on a regular basis with all of your team members. They won't feel the need to take things personally or be defensive. It will feel more like a coach pointing out how to run a play a little better in sports—that's just what coaches and players do and it's how teams and players elevate themselves to the next level of performance.

Formal feedback

The second forum for delivering feedback occurs in formal development processes such as performance reviews, career development programs, project reviews, and other similar mechanisms.

Beyond fulfilling any organizational requirements such as documenting performance through a company's review process, the purpose of delivering formal feedback is to take a step back on a regular basis and check in with the employee on how they are progressing with respect to their various performance and professional development goals.

The cadence for formal reviews is often set by the organization, as is the template for the review. Historically, it has been most common to have these reviews annually or every six months. Increasingly, organizations are leaning away from annual/bi-annual performance reviews in favor of more frequent (and slightly less formal) check-ins. This shift aligns with the trend of creating a "culture of feedback," which encourages people not to wait until these big checkpoints to have feedback discussions.

If you are given the power to choose, I recommend checking in formally on either a bi-annual or a quarterly basis. It doesn't make sense to have formal check-ins more frequently than that because it takes time for there to be enough data to support having a big-picture discussion. Also, depending on the number of direct reports you have, it can become very time-consuming to have to prepare for all of those formal discussions.

But if you don't have formal discussions at least once every six months, you miss the opportunity to help an employee make important course-corrections throughout the year. And many employees interpret infrequent reviews as a signal that their professional development and career progression are not a priority to you or to the wider organization.

Now let's discuss the key principles to keep in mind when giving formal feedback through a mechanism such as a performance review.

First and foremost, preparation is essential — and orders of magnitude more so than with ongoing feedback. This is because you are trying to provide an entire snapshot of a person's professional development in formal reviews, and a big part of how you successfully do that is through clear and precise language and tone. Not only that, but formal reviews are usually the basis for salary and promotion decisions, and they involve documentation that will be given to the employee and included in their personnel file.

For this reason, I strongly recommend iteration and rehearsal. Anything you write should be edited and re-edited. If you have a sensitive situation to deal with in a review, you may even want to run anything you write through your manager or a human resources professional to have an extra set of eyes on it. Practice what you plan to say multiple times before going into the discussion. Think through how you will strike the right tone and convey your points in an effective way. Even if you plan to deliver the document in advance or you intend to read through the document with the individual before engaging in a discussion about it, you'll want to think about how you will articulate certain points. Anticipate questions that may come up and contemplate how you would answer them.

People tend to scrutinize the performance reviews they receive, especially when the results of those reviews are tied to promotions, salary increases, and bonuses. Little things you may not have even intended to convey can get blown out of proportion in the mind of your employee and can create unwanted ripple effects. Iterating and rehearsing will help maximize your chances of having a successful discussion.

Some of you may be thinking to yourselves, *This seems like a lot of preparation; I don't think my managers have done this.* If that's the case, how did it make you feel to come out of a review where your manager didn't appear to have put much thought into it? If you are fortunate enough to have had a very positive experience with a manager who put time and care into your review, how did that make you feel by comparison?

Preparation is so important in demonstrating the value you place on your team members and their professional development. As a general guideline, plan to spend at least one hour writing each formal review and fifteen minutes preparing in advance for the discussion. But take as much time as it requires to do the job well.

Imagine you are a coach of a sports team and you're preparing your team for a game as you give them a locker room speech. In a similar way, the best reviews have a tone that says, "We're on the same side. I want to see you succeed." They articulate the ways a person can elevate their performance and they show that person that you are at their service to help them along the way.

Unlike ongoing reviews, it's more important to be in person for formal reviews if at all possible. A performance review is a big deal for most people; doing it in person conveys respect for both the employee and the event.

As you're going through the review, begin by painting the big picture and setting the overall tone of the review. If things are going well, make sure that's clear up front. If, on the whole, things are not so good, find the right way to communicate that.

As you step through the details of the review that follows, employ the SBIS framework wherever appropriate. Elaborate with specifics where needed. Pause frequently and ask questions that invite a dialog.

Do not nit-pick during formal reviews. Smaller issues should have come out during ongoing feedback sessions along the way. If you've done a good job delivering ongoing feedback, you will have already discussed much of what shows up in a performance review, and you will either be checking back in on progress, or you will be highlighting overall performance themes and goals going forward. Again, this is all about summarizing the most important elements for your team member's professional development.

Lastly, end with how you plan to support your team member's development going forward. Their development is a team effort, and you want them to know you are committed. Make it tangible and actionable so your team member can gauge your follow-through.

If you can check all of these boxes during a formal review, the chances are so much higher that your team member will walk away knowing exactly how they are doing, knowing what to do to elevate their performance to the next level, and recognizing that you are genuinely committed to their development. This is so essential in building loyalty and trust.

Common mistakes

Giving great feedback takes practice. If you employ the strategies and tactics we have discussed to this point, you will elevate your capability as a manager and a coach to a level reached by very few. But if you're new to this, don't sweat it if you don't nail it the first time. It takes repetition. Just do your best to implement the best practices we have discussed. And if you do make a mistake, learn from it, dust yourself off, and apply what you've learned the next opportunity you have to practice.

Here is a list of some of the mistakes people make with respect to giving feedback (and the way to correct for it):

- Trying to give too much feedback. (Don't nitpick; focus on important things and balance positive and negative feedback.)
- Judging the individual rather than the actions. (Comment on the behavior, not the person behind it.)
- Being too vague. (Use SBIS and ground things in real-world examples.)
- Speaking for other people. (Stick to your own observations.)
- Sandwiching constructive feedback between positive messages. (Don't water down constructive feedback with a "positive sandwich.")

- Exaggerating with generalities. (Stick to facts and clear observations.)
- Psychoanalyzing the motives behind the behavior. (Stick to discussing the observed behavior.)
- Going on too long. (Keep it concise and to the point. "Practice the pause." Ask questions. Make it a dialog.)
- Embedding an implied threat in the feedback. (Avoid anything that could be perceived as an implied threat.)
- Using humor that's out of place. (Avoid attempting to use humor to diffuse a situation. Stick to communicating facts and observations in a constructive or unemotional tone.)
- Delivering feedback as a question rather than a statement. (State your observations with confidence.)

Handling the unexpected in a feedback session

Occasionally, a person's reaction in a feedback session may escalate. They may become frustrated, upset, or angry. While this is rare, it can happen. Your primary objective is to hear that person out and de-escalate the situation as much as you can. Even if you are unable to de-escalate the situation, avoid doing anything that may escalate it. Here are some tips on how to handle a situation like this:

- Listen, listen, listen… then listen some more. Make sure your team member feels heard without siding in one direction or the other.
- Keep your emotions as neutral as possible and ask questions in a calm, unemotional tone.

- Take a break to regroup if things overheat.
- End the meeting in a calm, collected way, but be clear on timing for a follow up discussion.
- Use your peers, talk to your manager, or discuss the situation with a human resources professional to help identify the best way to address the issue (unless the employee has asked for confidentiality).

Asking for feedback on yourself

It's a great thing if you genuinely want to understand how you can improve as a manager. It stands to reason that the best source of this information would come from those whom you are managing.

Yes and no. They may have great feedback. But even the most approachable managers still have the power dynamic to contend with. Most people will filter what they say to their manager. That is one of the reasons 360 review processes exist—they theoretically provide a more protected and anonymous way for subordinates and peers to give unfiltered feedback to a manager. (But 360 review processes have their weaknesses, including the fact that they tend to include forced-choice questionnaires that can miss the color that would come through in a straightforward conversation.)

All that being said, even filtered feedback from your direct reports can be valuable. It's tempting to invite feedback about yourself from an employee after you have given feedback to them, such as at the end of a formal review.

But through experience, I have learned it is best to keep formal reviews and feedback discussions focused on the individual. They are the man-/woman-of-the-hour and that time should be all about them and their professional development. They deserve that. The only time to reference yourself is by asking what you could be doing to better support their development. But even when you do that, try not to take things down the path where the conversation shifts to being primarily about you. Most employees won't want it to go there anyway. And chances are you will be catching them off guard, so they likely won't be prepared to provide a good answer anyway.

When it comes to soliciting feedback about yourself as a manager, schedule a separate one-on-one session with each individual you would like to provide you with their feedback. Give them an overview of why you want their input and the type of feedback you would like to receive. Invite them to be as open and honest with you as possible and share with them the value you place on their input. Stress to them that their openness and honesty will help you get better, which is your primary goal. All of this will give them time to prepare for the discussion, which is an essential ingredient to making this work.

Some questions that work well to solicit useful feedback under these circumstances are:

- Do you have any feedback for me?
- How can I support you better in specific projects/work streams/tasks?
- What was one thing your last manager did that you liked that I don't do?
- What is one thing that I can do differently?
- Is there anything I should start doing? Stop doing? What do I do that you would prefer I not do?

Again, you can send questions like this and other topics in advance to give the person a chance to prepare what they want to say and how they want to say it.

Lastly, if you are truly committed to getting the best feedback possible from your direct reports, you can also replicate some of the benefits of a 360 process on your own by asking an intermediary to gather feedback from your team about you. This intermediary could be your manager or a peer who is willing to take the time to do so. The primary benefit of an intermediary is that they add a layer of anonymity that can make some people more comfortable in sharing open, honest, and direct feedback. But for that to be the case, you'll want to select an intermediary you believe stands the best chance of soliciting the most honest feedback possible.

If you want to give this approach a try, it's best if you make the intermediary's job as easy as possible since you are asking them to take time out of their schedule to help you. One thing you can do is outline a series of prompting questions the intermediary can use in the discussions. (It's fine if they want to go off script, but your preparation shows them that this is important to you and that you are respectful of their time.) It's also good if you can take the lead on scheduling the discussions on behalf of all the people involved and handling any other logistics.

Just like sessions you lead by yourself, talk to people in advance or send out information that lets everyone know what you are hoping to achieve, details to help them prepare and reduce the burden on them, and a sincere thank you for taking time out of their schedule to help you develop.

In closing

Great managers are outstanding teachers. They place tremendous emphasis on coaching and developing employees. This is the foundation for building a superior team.

We have unpacked this topic and explored it from a wide variety of angles. It's a lot to digest, and it will take time to assimilate it and implement it. But it's worth the effort. Mastering this area of management will set you apart from so many other managers and leaders. Depending on how much professional experience you already have by this point, you can likely attest to this from your own experience working with the different types of managers you have had in the past. Great managers who are skilled at coaching seem to be the exception, not the rule.

Be the exception. You have the tools. Pair it with the appetite to succeed through these principles, and you are on the path to greatness.

Chapter 6:

Tailoring Your Management Style

So much has been written throughout the years about what makes leaders and managers great at what they do. Embedded within these efforts to encapsulate greatness are an attempt to describe the ideal profile of such a person, as though great leadership always comes in one form.

But time and again, these descriptions fall short and fail to capture what you find in the real world. They are too one-dimensional. There simply aren't universals in something as varied as leading teams and organizations of people in the dynamic environment we work in.

This is why a CEO can be a tremendous success at one time and place, but he or she fails to move the needle in another. It's why a manager may hit a home run in one situation and miss entirely in another.

This is one of the reasons adaptability is a key characteristic of great managers. Everything is constantly changing and shifting, and every situation is unique. For managers to succeed in a sustainable way, they must be flexible and adaptable.

Nowhere is this truer than with respect to the art and science of managing people. Every individual is unique, as is every situation in which that individual finds themselves. When you combine a unique individual with a unique situation, you have an almost infinite set of possible circumstances that may require distinct and nuanced ways of approaching them. True wisdom does not always appear one way. Neither does superior management. Sometimes a situation calls for patience; other times it calls for urgency. Sometimes it calls for forceful action; other times it calls for yielding.

Over the years, I have heard one question come up in job interviews for manager positions more times than I can count: "What is your leadership/management style?" The truth of the matter is that the person who would be best suited for the position is almost always the one who could honestly answer, "My style depends on the situation." But baked into the question is the presumption that a leader/manager has one general approach and that the approach is either a strong one or a weak one.

To become a top-tier manager, your journey is not really about honing *your way* of managing. Yes, you will mature and develop your styles and approaches (plural) over time, but you'll also always be learning, adapting, and adjusting. There is no one-size-fits-all approach that is effective. Cookie-cutter management doesn't work. The micromanager follows a cookie-cutter approach, and we all know that the micromanager is limited. The always-hands-off manager suffers from a different flavor of the same issue— they are two sides of the same coin.

It's far better to aim for mastering the ability to tailor your managerial/leadership approach to the individual and situation. That is a difficult task, because unlike the one-size-fits-all manager, you won't be leaning on guidelines you can abide by at all times. At most, you'll have rules of thumb to steer you, which we will discuss in a bit. And instead of learning and honing a specific managerial technique or approach, your path will be that of honing your instincts, your intuition, your powers of observation, and your emotional intelligence.

Many theories of management have been proposed over the years to identify what good management is and to give people guidance on how to deal with the many situations a manager faces. In my experience, it is best to hold these lightly because of the reasons of uniqueness we have discussed. But to give you a feel for the types of adjustments you'll want to make to your approach based on the individual and the circumstance, we will focus on three dimensions that yield some rules of thumb for how you may want to adapt your style. The three dimensions are:

1. How competent the individual is (as it pertains to the given task, project, etc.)
2. How confident the individual is in their abilities (as it pertains to that task, project, etc.)
3. The degree to which they desire autonomy versus oversight/support/structure

All three of these can vary based on a person's stage of development, and it is often the case that a person moves through somewhat predictable stages as they take on tasks and work streams that are new to them. But with that being said, every task creates a new situation for a given individual that may or may not translate into predictable behaviors, and likewise, an individual's personality may color how they act in a given circumstance more than their experience level.

Competence

Competence is the most obvious and straightforward dimension when it comes to adapting one's style to the individual and the situation.

When somebody is new to a task, we expect them to be a beginner. It is natural that they are low on the spectrum of competence with respect to that task. That's the time it is usually best as a manager to be more directive. Get hands on. Spend ample time showing the individual how you want things done. Chances are you will want to be making the key decisions that come up along the way. And throughout your oversight of the process, it is good practice to constantly check for understanding.

As a person comes up the competence curve on a task and becomes moderately competent, you can start to back away to a degree and give them more independence. Your goal is to empower that employee to succeed so that you only need to provide hands-on help when it is truly needed. For example, you may begin reducing the frequency or depth of your check-ins as you move from being directive to suggesting refinements. Decision-making can become collaborative at this stage. It's useful to keep the ball in the other person's court by asking lots of open-ended questions and looking to them to provide you with recommended solutions to problems. As often as you can, ask them, "What would you do?"

When a person has high competence, your goal shifts to providing the maximum level of autonomy possible. When they reach this point, you will want to allow that person to take the lead and form their own perspectives. Check-ins become more about keeping you informed in the key areas you need to be involved in as a manager. You will also want to be looking for additional ways to challenge the individual, taking them beyond what they thought was possible and guiding them toward true mastery.

All of us are constantly moving through these stages of competence in various areas of work. Because of our natural talents, our experiences, and our level of enthusiasm for various tasks, we will find ourselves at different points along the spectrum on different skills and tasks. For example, an individual may be highly competent with skills and tasks involving written communication, while being a beginner on skills and tasks involving verbal communication. And every time we "move up"—whether it's taking on larger tasks or stepping into new roles—we find ourselves back to being relative beginners.

Remember that competence applies to every aspect of a person's professional life—not only to projects and tasks, but to professional skills as well. An entry-level knowledge worker likely starts out as a beginner with respect to email etiquette and technique. One manager I coached who led a customer-facing team asked every new team member to send her a copy of an email before they sent it out to a customer so that she could provide feedback. She said that it usually took people one or two months before they were ready to send emails without her input, and even after that, many people would continue sending her the highly sensitive emails to have an extra set of eyes on them.

Confidence

The next dimension that offers some generalizable rules of thumb for adapting your managerial style is the confidence level a person has in themselves with respect to a given area of work. The intersection between a person's competence and confidence is the basis for a theory first introduced in 1969 by Paul Hersey and Ken Blanchard called the "Life cycle theory of leadership," which later evolved into what is known today as "Situational Leadership." Below is a graphic adapted from this theory.

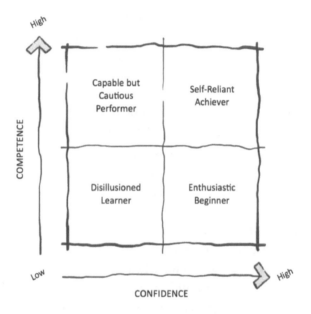

Taking a step back to assess your team's varied development stage, enables you to understand how to support them most effectively and get more leverage.

Like competence, a person's confidence in their abilities tends to shift over time as they gain experience. But unlike competence, which tends to start low and gradually become higher over time, confidence does not always follow that path.

In fact, part of the original situational leadership theory is that, when given a task that is entirely new to a person, that person may be low on competence but may begin with very high confidence, approaching it with an attitude of "I've got this." This person would fall into the "enthusiastic beginner" category in the graphic above. In a sense, they don't know what they don't know.

It's not the case that every single person will start at this point. But when somebody does, it creates a unique situation for the manager. Because the person is new to the task, you will need to be more directive. But the individual may not think they need that level of direction because their confidence is so high. They may resist oversight. They may go off on their own and disappear for longer than expected as they wrestle with the task.

What usually happens next is that the person begins to recognize that they didn't know what they didn't know. Their confidence level then falls more in line with their competence level, placing them in the "disillusioned learner" category in the graphic above. At this stage, the two of you will likely be more on the same page with respect to providing them with the direction and support they need. You can work with them as the beginner they are by leading with your ideas, explaining your rationale, being hands-on and so forth. But it is important to offer praise and demonstrate you care throughout this coaching. After all, you want them not only to grow in ability, but you'll want their confidence to climb back up accordingly.

For the individual whose confidence exceeds their competence, try to be somewhat delicate — your job is not to "put them in their place." That being said, you will want to consistently provide feedback according to the principles we discussed in the last chapter, since this is the most expeditious and effective way to boost their self-awareness while also bringing them up the learning curve on the task at hand.

You will come to see that not everyone finds themselves in a position where confidence exceeds competence. Some people tend to lack self-confidence, so their confidence may consistently lag behind their ability level in a given area. Others may start out highly confident, but after having a rude awakening and realizing how little they know, their confidence can be bruised and remain low even as their capabilities rise.

Both of these situations result in the "capable but cautious performer." When somebody's confidence remains low (or variable) even while their competence level is progressing nicely, one of your jobs is to listen, encourage, and help that person believe in themselves. This is crucial because somebody who lacks confidence will not act in an empowered, autonomous way. They will exhibit behaviors such as continuing to look to you to sign off on everything even when it's no longer necessary.

During this time, praise becomes more important than ever. Positive feedback using the SBIS framework is highly effective because it is rooted in a factual observation that a person lacking confidence will find it difficult to refute. And with enough objective evidence, their confidence will grow.

Once the person reaches the point where competence is high and their confidence matches it, they are in the sweet spot of a "self-reliant achiever." Again, you want to keep elevating that person and taking them to heights they didn't realize were possible. And this is the time to stretch them again, giving them new tasks or larger work streams and moving them back to the stage of beginner in those areas.

Desired autonomy

The third dimension that has practical implications for how you tailor your management approach is the degree to which somebody has a preference for autonomy versus a preference for structure and oversight.

This dimension can correlate with competence and confidence, but it can also be an independent factor that relates more to the individual, their personality, and their comfort operating in situations where there is ambiguity.

First, let's take a look at the extremes.

On one extreme end of the spectrum, you have the overly independent person. Their approach tends to be, "I can figure this out." This can be a great attitude provided the person truly can handle it on their own and they still check in with you to the degree you want. But watch out for this attitude if a person is too low on the competence scale. You could end up giving them too much rope and things could go off the rails.

On the other extreme end of the spectrum, you have the overly dependent person or the over-sharer. This person tends to want to check in with you at every step along the way. Often, they want you to provide them with structure and guidance on everything, or they look to you to sign off on every small decision they are making as they execute their work. This may be perfectly appropriate when somebody is in the beginner phase on a project. But if it persists beyond the point at which they are clearly able to act with more independence, you may be in a danger zone. Things could slow down and progress could come to a halt while they wait for your input. Likewise, your own bandwidth may become stretched by attending to that person's needs.

For the most part, it's fine to let people work the way they want to—this will help you get the best out of them. Some people simply operate better when they have the freedom to figure things out and they can come to you only when they need you. Others may gain comfort by quickly running things through you even when you recognize there isn't as much of a need. There is value in adapting your style to align with those desires.

Just beware of the danger zones that can come about when somebody tips too far in one direction or the other relative to where they need to be from a development perspective. That's the time when you will want to nudge them more toward the middle of this spectrum.

In summary

The three dimensions of competence, confidence, and autonomy are helpful to consider when establishing an appropriate cadence of check-ins with a team member.

For example, if a person is likely to veer off course on a piece of work given their current competence level, you will save yourself considerable time and energy if you check in with them early and often. The longer you wait, the more effort is required to get back on track, just like the time it takes to recover from a mistake in a pilot's flight path increases with each additional minute the pilot remains off course.

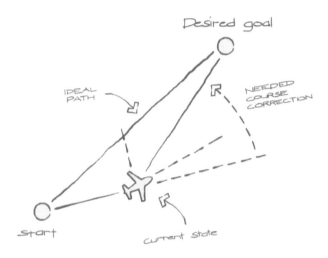

Making small tweaks and pivots to project direction through regular check-ins will avoid major changes and lost time in the future.

While competence, confidence, and autonomy are important dimensions to consider, they are by no means the be-all and end-all when it comes to tailoring your approach to the individual's needs in a situation.

A team member could be going through a personal challenge at home such as a divorce or family illness, and suddenly they need more flexibility than usual. An interpersonal conflict could arise with a team member who is working on a particular task, and you need to step in and get engaged in a situation you normally wouldn't need to be involved in. A team member could be knocking it out of the park but be struggling to overcome a key stakeholder's perspective regarding their ability level, and you may need to help them with a plan to elevate their "personal brand." The list of possible situations you may face as a manager is limitless.

But you are adaptable. You are committed to looking at every situation with fresh eyes and the openness to approaching it in a nuanced way.

And when you do that, not only are you more effective as a manager, but you expand the trust and loyalty that exists between you and your team. This is one more thing that further cements you on your journey to becoming a truly great manager.

Chapter 7:

Motivating and Inspiring Your Team

At this point, we have delved into much of the "how-to" of great management—setting goals and expectations, prioritizing, delegating, coaching and providing feedback, and tailoring your style to fit with the needs of the situation.

But what makes a manager truly stand out in people's minds is combining the mastery of the skills and capabilities we have discussed with something more emotional. Great managers are inspiring. Great managers are people you want to be around because of how they make you feel. Great managers motivate you to be your best.

Feeling motivated is wonderful. It makes the work we do enjoyable. It helps us access the sought-after "flow states" we wish to harness more in our lives. And practically speaking, it is a key component to sustained performance of the individual and the team.

The reality, however, is that motivation levels on your team will naturally ebb and flow, just as they do in your own life. A big aspect of your job as a manager is to bring out the best in your team members as much as possible so they give you, their team, and the organization as a whole their best. Together, you are trying to learn, to grow, and to achieve your collective and individual goals. All goal achievement is rooted in change. That's what accomplishing a goal is at a fundamental level—it's changing something for the better.

But change doesn't usually come easily, even for people who are oriented toward change. That's why the entire field of "change management" exists. Change for an individual requires overcoming the status quo and reaching new heights. Driving change at the team and organizational levels compounds the complexity by orders of magnitude.

There are three things to focus on to successfully drive change among your team members:

First, you need to *capture their hearts*. An individual has to want the change at an emotional level. That never happens at the level of "what," it only happens at the level of "why." To capture the hearts of team members, you need to tie the specific change to the bigger picture, to deeper rationale, or to the overriding mission. In a sense, there needs to be *a cause* that people can rally behind. That goes not only for tying it to the team's mission or the organization's mission at hand, but also to the individual's mission. How does it help them? Why is it important for them?

Second, you need to *capture their minds*. What are you looking for an individual to do? What is being asked of them has to be clear and precise as well as tangible and actionable. Now we are operating at the level of "what" needs to happen and "how" it needs to get done, both of which need to be rooted in the underpinning logic and rationale (ideally supported by data). To capture people's minds, the reason for the change must have clear rationale and the way you plan to go about it must make logical sense.

Finally, you want to *align performance criteria and incentives* with the change. In other words, after capturing hearts and minds, you capture their wallets. This is a practical step in pairing an individual's personal/professional motivations with the change at hand. This step is almost always insufficient without also capturing the hearts and minds, yet it's the one many leaders default to first. On the flip side, sometimes capturing hearts and minds alone is enough to spark the motivation to change if a person is mission-driven or sees it as a special opportunity for professional development.

But it's important to keep in mind that people come to work because they need to make a living and hopefully they want to advance professionally as well. It's important that we address both of these needs or they will feel taken advantage of in time. And when it comes to motivating people and driving change, it's crucial to demonstrate to people that they are valued and will be rewarded fairly through appropriately aligning compensation and career progression.

It's also important to mention that if incentives are misaligned, that becomes an outright barrier to driving the change you desire. Years ago, I worked with a company experiencing gross margin deterioration. They had put all kinds of initiatives in place to try to improve gross margins, including material cost reduction programs, supplier negotiation initiatives, and so forth. But their biggest problem turned out to be simple: their sales team was incentivized based on revenue only and had been discounting prices to compete with a new low-price entrant in the market. Once sales incentives were overhauled and reps were compensated based on hitting gross margin targets, they began focusing their efforts on higher-margin customer segments and the situation stabilized.

Great managers are fantastic agents of change. But motivating and inspiring teams to perform at their best takes even more than this. Ask a hundred people what makes an outstanding leader, and you will find an unmistakable theme emerge—outstanding leaders lead by example.

As a world class manager, leading by example means one thing above all else: Being a "player-coach." How do you become an outstanding player-coach?

Get your hands dirty

Player-coaches dive in and get their hands dirty. They don't just stand on the sidelines and coach; they get out on the field and play alongside their team. Arm-chair managers, on the other hand, sit back behind their desk and lead from a distance. Arm-chair managers do not inspire teams to go above and beyond. Worse yet, their behavior creates indifference and can even spark resentment. They are the reason many employees are under the illusion that taking a management role means that you get to sit back and relax.

Destroy that misconception among your team! When your team members know you are willing to get in the trenches and fight the good fight alongside them, they will want to perform for you. That doesn't mean spending all of your time in the trenches with them. They want room and space to breathe, too. But a willingness to dive into the trenches goes a long way.

Tim Denning of *The Startup* shared how influential it was when his former boss, a highly paid senior executive, told him, "I'll never ask you to do something I'm not prepared to do myself." This wasn't an empty statement, either. Tim went on to share stories of how his boss backed that up through his actions, such as staying on the phones all night during a crisis when the company's IT systems were crashing.

This is powerful leadership, and it inspires your team to perform at its best.

Act the way you want others to act

Leading by example fundamentally means behaving the way you want other people to behave. Elevate the game through your own actions. Think of how Serena Williams changed the entire way women's tennis was played. Or how the late Kobe Bryant was famous for showing up hours before everyone else to take practice shots before a game.

There can be no "do as I say, not as I do" if you want to inspire people. Drew Houston from Dropbox tells a funny story about how he was once a couple minutes late to an all-employee meeting about the importance of being on time. While not necessarily funny to him at the time, he points out that many of us have to learn the hard way that it's the things you do that people notice the most, not the things you say.

So be a role model. Show people what great looks like.

Collaborate, collaborate, collaborate

The best managers and leaders are known to be highly collaborative. It's not always their way or the highway. They recognize they are fallible. They understand the power of consensus and team-based decision-making.

So, bring people on your team into the decision-making process. Do so even in situations you might not otherwise think of involving somebody. Expose them to situations beyond their level. Ask for their opinion on topics before forming your own opinion, even if in the end you have to make a unilateral decision. If you do these things, people will feel valued. They may feel honored as well.

Yes, at times collaboration can feel like it slows things down or it adds an unnecessary step to the process. At times collaboration can be difficult. But it's vital to well-functioning teams and organizations. And it boils down to regularly using just four simple words: "What do you think?"

I once witnessed a fantastic example of this in a meeting with the CEO of a large public corporation and his executive team. We were preparing for a critical meeting with the board of directors regarding a proposed acquisition, and the group of senior executives couldn't agree on how to best describe the target company's brand. They went back and forth for thirty minutes debating the issue amongst themselves. Finally, the CEO cut off the conversation and singled out the most junior person in the room—a quiet analyst whose only reason for being in the room was to take notes and help make changes to the presentation materials following the meeting. "I've heard all these other people's opinions, but what do you think?" he asked. The analyst looked stunned, but after a moment he cleared his throat and shared his thoughts. The CEO nodded his head and said, "I like it. I think we should go with it." The analyst's sense of pride was palpable, and every other time I was in a meeting with him from that point on, I saw him come out of his shell more and more and share his valuable insights.

Empower people

Steve Jobs once said that if you want to retain good people, you have to show them you trust them. And when you *give* trust, you *earn* it as well.

Always look for ways to further empower a member of your team beyond where they are today. As we've discussed, it helps give you more bandwidth. But it also motivates them. Research in career satisfaction has shown that attaining mastery is one of the strongest predictors of career satisfaction. Similarly, autonomy has been demonstrated to be one of the primary factors that drives intrinsic motivation. By empowering people to achieve a level of mastery, ownership and independence, you will fuel them to give their best and they will enjoy the work they do that much more.

Empowerment can be about little things. Ask your team what they think. Ask them for recommendations. When they present problems, ask them for their ideas about how to solve the problem so that they become more solution-oriented. Allow them to make decisions. Top talent wants to have an impact at work. Top talent wants to be in a position of decision-making. If you want to retain top talent, help elevate them with respect to decision-making.

Years ago, I worked with a German-born CEO of a large water disinfection company who was a master of this type of empowerment. Although he often knew the answer to a question, Christian would always ask others' opinions first, and if they were off-base, he would artfully redirect and coach in a way that made his employees feel ownership over their answer. One simple approach he used was to follow up an employee's comments with, "I agree, now how would you think about *this*?" His emphasis on "*this*" was his way of pointing out a critical assumption they might have missed, while still giving them credit for their good thinking. This made employees feel trusted, empowered, and supported by Christian.

Show empathy

By now you are probably spotting a trend. A big part of inspiring and motivating people is about embodying the essential characteristics of great managers that we discussed in chapter two. Indeed, *who you are* is as important as *how you operate* as a manager.

Sometimes people want to succeed for themselves. Sometimes they want to succeed because of something beyond themselves, like a bigger mission.

And sometimes, people simply want to succeed because of you. They want to pull through for *you*. They want to make *you* proud.

That only happens when you have a strong and loyal relationship. Those types of working relationships are rooted in empathy. When we feel appreciated and that someone understands where we are coming from, we return favors. We look for ways to pay back for the small gifts we receive. And we tend to want to do more than is expected of us.

Show your team you have their best interests in mind. Demonstrate your appreciation through your comments and actions. Eat lunch with your team. Take people out for a cup of coffee and spend time getting to know them. The little things matter. Trust takes time to build, but if people see that you are coming from a genuine place, trust will naturally grow, and motivation and inspiration will follow.

Give credit, take blame

In victory, lead from behind. In crisis, lead from the front.

When bad things happen, take the blame. This means admitting when you are wrong, of course. It also means providing "air cover" for your team members as appropriate.

But go beyond that as well. Nothing will build loyalty and respect more than team members watching you take the bullet for them in tough times. Even if something wasn't "your fault," look for any way in which you could have prevented the situation from happening or mitigated it somehow. Yes, you might be relying on the clarity that comes from hindsight, but there is always *something* you could have done. By focusing on that when you discuss the situation with your team, you are demonstrating what accountable leaders do—they always take ownership and look for how they might have handled a situation in a more optimal way.

I once had the opportunity to meet the former NFL quarterback Steve Young, and he articulated this principle perfectly when he described what he called the "mitigating quarterback." Young explained that when the mitigating quarterback is part of a bad play, he will follow it up with "the tight end didn't block," "the wide receiver ran the wrong route," "it was because of the wind," or any other reason that focuses the blame on circumstances beyond the quarterback's control. But a professional and accountable quarterback will take ownership of a bad play even in the case where he threw a good pass. Young went on to say that nobody likes playing for a mitigating quarterback. People want to play for the professional, accountable quarterback and team leader.

So be the accountable quarterback. Step up and take the heat for the shortfall. Of course, that doesn't mean you should ignore where your team fell short. If there is an opportunity to give feedback, then it's important to do that at the right time and in the appropriate environment. But own it when things don't go well and look out for your team whenever possible.

Likewise, when good things happen, be generous in giving the credit for the team's accomplishments to your team. Even if you drove the success or you were the deciding factor, great leaders don't focus on themselves as individuals. Every win is the team's win. There is nothing more corrosive to loyalty than a manager who takes the credit for their team's accomplishments. But a manager who genuinely gives credit to their team fosters loyalty, and doing so never takes away from that manager's own success.

So, inspire people by how generously you give your team credit and through the strength you display by taking the blame and criticism on your team's behalf.

Praise early and often

Be liberal with your praise. Thank people for their work. Show people that their contribution matters. The human voice has an important encouraging and reinforcing effect. It seems like such an obvious point, yet it's a small and easy thing that so many managers and leaders fail to do. And guess what? People feel used. They feel uninspired. The motivation bleeds out of their system.

But genuine praise lifts people up. It helps them stay motivated.

While constructive feedback should always be delivered in a private conversation, praise can be given in public as well as in private. Public praise often amplifies its effect. People feel good when they are publicly recognized. Giving genuine praise is one of the most enjoyable parts of your job as a manager, and it truly benefits your team members as well, so give that gift generously.

In summary

It's exciting to arrive at this point, because we've now put the essential pieces of greatness together. Master the skills and techniques of managerial effectiveness. Embrace the characteristics that make you the kind of person who wins the hearts and minds of those around you. Do these things and you will inspire people through your leadership.

Chapter 8:

Managing Laterally and Managing Up

U p until this point, we have focused all of our attention on the ways you interface with your team in your capacity as a manager. Indeed, that is the central aspect of your role, and if you're new to management, it's appropriate for that to be your primary area of focus in the earliest part of your journey.

But now we're going to flip everything on its head. Because the mere fact of your being in a managerial role means it's more crucial than ever for you to focus a greater portion of your time and attention on how you engage with the people beside you and above you—what we will refer to as "managing laterally" and "managing up." So, let's discuss why this is so important and how to go about it in the most effective way possible.

Managing laterally

When you are a manager, your natural tendency is to want to spend all your time with your team. After all, that's where progress primarily happens on the things for which you are accountable. Collectively, you and your team are getting the job done that you were all hired to do.

If you have been promoted recently into the position, you are likely finding that being a manager is more demanding than you expected. People need your input, your approval, your sign-off, your support, and fundamentally your *time and attention* if things are to keep moving forward. Again, this adds to the feeling of needing to be with your team as much as possible.

But a complicating factor enters the situation. When you're in a management role of any type, you've reached a point in your career where you are also going to be tugged at by a bunch of new priorities that do not involve your day-to-day activities with your team. You'll have new meetings to attend, new committees or working groups where you need to represent your function—all of which eats into the time you have to spend with your team.

In fact, based on my own experience, with every level you rise in the organizational hierarchy (i.e., from manager to director, from director to vice president, from vice president to the C-suite), I have personally found that the pace doubles and the bandwidth you have available to spend with your team on day-to-day work execution gets cut in half due to new responsibilities and commitments.

This compounds the uncomfortable feeling that you are not spending enough time with your team.

But here's the rub. Now it is more important than ever that you spend a big portion of your time engaging with people outside your team. Indeed, a larger part of your role than you may realize has to do with you personally engaging with your colleagues across functions.

One of my mentors once recommended, "When you get to the levels where you are managing teams, you should be spending more time with people outside your team than with your team." I remember it seemed unfathomable. How could he suggest something so extreme?

But think about it this way—you are ultimately responsible for your team's success. You are the tip of the spear. There is nobody on your team who is better positioned to be the one out there championing your cause, communicating your progress, securing support, driving alignment across functions, and ensuring your objectives are properly resourced.

Don't get hung up on whether you should be spending more than 50 percent of your time with people outside of your team. The specific number isn't important, and the actual time you spend will ebb and flow based on your role, the situation you are in, and other factors. The point is that there is a lot for you to do outside of working with your team. It is a critical role for you to play, and it's a role you simply can't delegate.

The larger the organization, the more important this role becomes. Large organizations suffer more acutely from silos, and there tends to be a bigger risk of things falling through the cracks due to lack of alignment. Ask any head of a function what their goals are, and they may give you a solid scorecard that lines up nicely with their functional responsibilities. Now, take a look at your own objectives and see how well they tie into that person's scorecard. There's a good chance you won't be able to find a direct connection with some of those goals. And I'm certain you will find that at least one of your key priorities shows up way down on their list of goals as almost an afterthought.

The only way you are going to accomplish your goals as a team is if you personally take charge through managing laterally on a consistent basis. Constantly interface with people in other groups. Understand what they are trying to achieve. Make sure they know what you are working on and why. Seek to understand *who* on their team is running point on anything related to your team's projects and objectives. Create solid working relationships and rapport so that when issues arise, discomfort or awkwardness won't stand in the way of working through the problems. When you do raise issues, do so as quickly as possible, but always do so in a diplomatic way. Ask how you can help them and make sure you are doing what you can to support their goals personally and through the efforts of your team.

Managing up

The essence of managing up is the same for an individual contributor as it is for the leader of a huge organization: You want to make your manager's life easier. If you do that, you both win. If you can make your manager look good (and everyone above you, for that matter), everyone wins. Many successful careers were built by following through on that very basic principle. After all, who wouldn't want to have a person around them who makes them look good? Who wouldn't want to find ways to give that individual more opportunities and greater responsibility? That's how you become a linchpin in the eyes of your superiors.

Perhaps that's the reason you're in a management position in the first place. You understand this, or you did it naturally as an individual contributor.

As a manager, the same principle still applies. The key difference is that managing up takes on a new level of precedence when you reach a managerial level in the organization. As an individual contributor, you were only responsible for yourself when you communicated progress, flagged issues, and so on. But now you are doing this on behalf of a team of people. It's a bigger responsibility.

Put yourself in your manager's shoes and think about what they want most during your interactions. This becomes easier when you yourself are a manager, since you have the experience of sitting on that side of the table and comparing and contrasting the ways in which your team members manage up with you.

In general, your manager cares about four things:

1. Major issues that they need to know about
2. The status of key projects or work streams
3. Resourcing/bandwidth challenges
4. How your team is doing

You don't need to cover every one of these in every single check-in. Major issues come first and trump everything else. Don't wait for a scheduled check-in when significant issues arise. You will build trust by openly communicating about problems as soon as they occur. You always want your manager to hear about issues from you before they hear about them from other people, if possible. Even if you don't have all of the details, you can still give your manager a heads-up immediately by saying, "I just heard about this issue. I don't know the full scope of the situation yet, but I am on it and as soon as I have the details, I will loop you in."

If the status of your work streams looks good and there aren't any new resourcing/bandwidth challenges, a quick communication to let your manager know that will suffice. Most managers prefer to spend time diving into where things are off track, why, and what can be done to mitigate issues.

Lastly, you don't need to take time in every check-in to talk about how your team is doing. Most likely, your manager will ask about this periodically, and it will come up during the performance review cadence as well. If a new issue arises, then bring it to your manager's attention (e.g., performance issue, morale concerns, etc.). Otherwise, no news is good news. The same applies with respect to how you are doing.

Unless your manager has specified a clear preference or requirement, aim for a weekly pulse check with your manager and fill them in on any important updates that arise in between on an as-needed basis.

If a crisis arises, then it goes without saying that your frequency of check-ins will be a lot higher. You may be talking to your manager daily or even multiple times a day. Over-communicate. Even if it's just a brief update at the end of the day to tell them there is nothing new to report, you don't ever want your manager to feel like they are in the dark or that you've gone silent. Your primary goal is to give them confidence that the situation is in good hands, and to arm them with information so they aren't caught flat-footed when their superiors or peers come to them looking for information.

Beyond these essentials, there are three more principles to discuss with respect to a strong practice of managing up:

No matter what the issue is, don't be afraid to talk about it.

Open communication is the foundation of trusting relationships. Act the way you would want your team members acting with you. It can be tempting to hold something close to the vest until you have it under control. But this rarely pays off and it often backfires. Be transparent.

Never come empty-handed; always come prepared.

Treat your manager's time with respect.

The best way to be respectful of their time is to prepare for every interaction. Avoid coming to them with general questions or with problems. You want to be solution-oriented. That doesn't always mean you have to have a solution, but at least come to them having already tried a few things before asking for help. As a simple example, instead of saying, "I've been having trouble with something," say, "I've been working to identify a better way to…."

Execute and circle back.

The other way to demonstrate respect for your manager's time is to take the time to internalize any feedback or support they offer you. You may not always agree with everything, but search for the nugget of truth in anything they share. Execute on their recommendations and circle back with them to make sure you've done so correctly and to demonstrate to them that you have taken their suggestions to heart.

Managing up with multiple bosses, dotted lines and stakeholders

One additional challenge managers may face—one that is becoming increasingly common as organizational structures become more flat, fluid and/or matrixed—is that of navigating a situation where you report to multiple bosses or have dotted-line reporting. It can be tricky to navigate a situation where you or your team receives strong leadership influence from various senior stakeholders in addition to your direct manager.

For starters, it's very easy to feel pulled in lots of different directions, especially when those stakeholders are not on the same page. It can also be more difficult to manage your time and priorities because it's common for one stakeholder to demand more of your time or attention than others.

This is a frequent subject of griping among less-mature managers because it seemingly makes the job harder.

But my recommendation here is to reframe your situation. True, it may make the job more challenging, but it makes you that much more of linchpin because you are the only person who occupies your particular nexus of the organization. These groups and stakeholders come together through you.

Misalignment is unavoidable in organizations. The minute there is an organizational structure of any type, there are boundaries. Where there are boundaries, things will fall through the cracks. This is especially the case in large organizations, but it happens in organizations of any size.

When you are reporting to multiple people, you represent the point at which two or more functions or groups need to come together successfully for the organization to achieve its objectives. You might think of yourself as a quarterback when it comes to offense—you need to coordinate and bring together the disparate groups to a common objective. But you are also the free safety on defense, in many ways acting as the last line of defense when things slip through the cracks.

As for how to succeed in that role, the single most important thing for you to do is to prioritize frequent, clear communication to all stakeholders.

When you or your team has too many priorities competing for your time, you need to be the driver behind bringing the stakeholders together to collectively work through prioritization.

When misalignment arises between groups, you need to be the glue. Do not take for granted that the stakeholders you report to talk to each other. It's often the case that each will learn about the other stakeholders' priorities through you.

Any time you identify important disconnects, make it your job to solve them. Flag issues and break down the barriers by getting people in a room or onto a call to work through misalignment. Act as the objective, strategic, diplomatic person who sits between the groups and has an eye toward what's best for the overall organization.

While there is no sugar-coating how difficult a position it can be, take pride in the fact that you've been trusted to play this important and challenging role.

In summary

Being a manager is no easy task. Leading other people is a significant responsibility. But no matter how busy things become when managing a team, it's so important to carve out the time it takes to be successful in the other half of your job—engaging with peers and superiors. And that's a role that you simply can't delegate.

This is one key aspect of why it's so crucial to be a teacher and coach who empowers team members and helps them become more autonomous. The more independent your team becomes and the more they understand how they fit into the bigger picture, the more time you will have to devote to the important task of managing laterally and managing up.

Chapter 9:

Building an "A Team" —

Managing People In, Up, and Out

It can't be stressed enough—you are only as strong as the team you have supporting you. A weak team will hold you back. An outstanding team will have you punching well above your weight. And when you are surrounded by talented, hard-working individuals you enjoy being around, work can be a truly enjoyable and energizing experience.

By this point, we have explored many aspects of molding your team into a group of superstars through superior managerial and coaching skills. It's now time to add the final ingredient for building the "A team"— ensuring your team is composed of the right individuals.

Building an "A team"

We all recognize that some people are uniquely talented "A Players." They are intelligent and hard-working. They have the right attitude. They have the soft skills it takes to be successful. They work well with others and are a pleasure to be around. These individuals are your "go-to" people. No matter what you throw their way, they seem to be able to handle it like a pro and consistently exceed your expectations.

Contrast them with your "B Players." Your B Players are fine; they get the job done. But they don't usually over-deliver or exceed expectations. They often leave something to be desired.

And then there are the "C Players" — the people who actively hold you and your team back. Sometimes it's a lack of skill or capability. Other times they bring a toxicity into the equation. Either way, you can see how these individuals pose a real problem when it comes to your team successfully achieving the task at hand.

If you zoom out and look at most organizations, you will find that the 80/20 rule more or less applies to productive output when it comes to talent. (i.e., Twenty percent of people are responsible for 80 percent of the value being contributed to the organization, or alternatively, 20 percent of people drive 80 percent of the productivity improvement. Whether or not it is an exact 80/20 ratio in all situations, the disproportionate contribution of top talent is evident).

Ask anyone with decades of managerial and leadership experience and they will corroborate the staggering difference between top talent and everyone else. Whenever I ask experienced managers I am coaching how much more value their top talent adds relative to their middle performers, they tell me it's anywhere from two to five times as much value.

The most ruthless assessors of talent tend to be private equity companies. They know the value of their investment is driven most by the quality of talent they have in key roles, and they recognize the disproportionate value-add of top talent. Most private equity companies will classify people into A, B, and C Players, and often, people in the bottom two categories are moved out of the organization.

While we would all love to believe that effective training and coaching can boost anyone from where they are to the level of an A Player, we know that's not the case. Some people are able to make the jump. But others won't be able to get there regardless of how much time and energy we invest in their development.

When you are a manager, beyond coaching and talent, the other essential lever you have when building an outstanding team is the selection of the right individuals for the job. That means hiring the right individuals and moving individuals out of roles when things are not working out.

In fact, the higher you rise in leadership ranks, the more the focus of your job is to select the right talent for roles and build great teams. It's simple arithmetic. There's always just one of you, but as you step into larger roles, the number of people you are responsible for leading grows. Every time that ratio changes, you have less ability to personally impact the destiny of the team through direct interactions with people. The only way for you to succeed is to shift more and more of your attention to building a great team.

The optimal situation is, of course, to have a team of all A Players. This turns out to be exceedingly rare. To begin with, any team you take over is unlikely to begin with all A Players. You can improve certain people's performance to that level through coaching and development, but not everyone will get to the A Player level. And you can make changes to the composition of the team, but too much change could compromise your ability to execute in the here and now or it could lead to other undesirable consequences. The A Players you do have are inherently more upwardly and laterally mobile, so it's only a matter of time before they get pulled into other roles. And despite your best efforts, you may not be successful in filling every vacancy with an A Player.

Nevertheless, I encourage you to strive for building a team of all A Players. It may be rare to get all the way there, but it can be done and it's the right goal to set your sights on.

Talented individuals are undoubtedly the foundation of great teams, but there are other important components to get right when building an A Team as well.

First, even an incredibly talented person needs to be in a role that is well-suited to them for their gifts to shine. This comes down to matching an individual to a role that fits their capability, their interests, and their development needs.

Second, the best teams have a diversity of perspectives and skills. Everybody has strengths and weaknesses, and often the two are different sides of the same coin (e.g., somebody's urgency may be the reason for their productivity, but it may contribute to their lack of patience). It's ideal if your team blends together a wide variety of strengths that balance out each other's weaknesses. Some people may be strategic and great at working at the big-picture level. Other people may be outstanding at managing tactics and execution. Some may be fantastic communicators. Some may be quantitative and analytical. Some people may have a ton of experience within your particular domain or industry. Others may be new to the space, but they come with fresh perspectives. You want one person's strength to be able to compensate for another person's weakness in a pragmatic way. This leads to effective execution, problem solving, and decision-making as a team.

And the most important weaknesses to address through team composition are your own. Be honest about your strengths and weaknesses and pay particular attention to making sure you have people on your team who compensate for your weaknesses.

Filling in for your gaps isn't your only priority. You also want to be on the lookout for who on your team could be groomed to be your successor. As I mentioned earlier, not having someone to take over for you can be the reason you are delayed in moving into your next role.

Grooming a successor has the added benefit of giving you a "right hand" to lean on along the way. This isn't always possible based on the structure or composition of your team. But any time you have a vacancy to fill, that could be your opportunity to bring in somebody who could eventually step in for you when you take on a future role.

Hiring

Every open position you have represents an opportunity. You can approach filling it with the mindset of "we just need somebody to do that person's job." Or you can think about it as an opportunity to take a significant step toward building the team of your dreams. An opening gives you the opportunity to bring in fresh perspective and experience. It is an opportunity to fill critical gaps in skills or knowledge. It is an opportunity to think differently about how your team is organized and to structure it in a more effective way. It is an opportunity to improve the dynamics on your team. And as we just discussed, it is an opportunity to find a right-hand man/woman who can be a future successor.

Unfortunately, managers don't always view open positions in this way. They rush to fill the position because they need somebody to do the job that somebody else was doing, rather than taking a step back and evaluating if they should use it as an opportunity to rethink things in a more meaningful way. Not only that, but people extend this thinking into one of the most common hiring mistakes — trying to hire for a very specific experience profile, and failing to place adequate emphasis on the candidate's growth potential, emotional intelligence, soft skills, or any number of other critical factors that can boost the caliber of their team.

It's natural to want to find someone who can step in and do the job on day one. Theoretically, this makes things much easier for you. But time and again people learn things the hard way. Their search extends indefinitely because they're too narrow in how they have defined the profile of the ideal individual. Or they compromise on the wrong dimensions to recruit for very specific expertise that isn't as essential as they think it is.

You can train a person on the skills necessary to do a job. But it's a lot harder to train for things like growth potential, attitude, mindset, self-awareness, and the multitude of soft skills and intangibles that set the true stars apart from the masses. Very often, a person who does not have the perfect background but brings these other qualities to the table ends up being the better fit for the role. But that person is often passed up or isn't even part of the consideration set due to the search parameters established by the hiring manager and recruiters.

If building a great team is one of the most vital roles a manager plays (and it grows in importance the higher a person rises in an organization), and if hiring is the best opportunity to create a step change in the quality of a team, it stands to reason that managers would dedicate lots of their own time to the recruiting process when they are filling a role.

In practice, the opposite is more commonly the case. Many managers take the approach of trying to offload as much of the responsibility onto a recruiter or the human resources team. They want a good outcome, but they aren't willing put in the time to help ensure this is the case.

Please don't make this mistake. Bad hiring decisions are tremendously costly, and there is plenty of research that has been published over the years to corroborate that. The U.S. Department of Labor pegs the cost of a bad hire at more than 30 percent of the employee's first-year earnings. Many believe it is much higher. As CEO of Zappos, Tony Hsieh once estimated that bad hires had cost the company "well over one hundred million dollars." Even mediocre hiring decisions are a huge missed opportunity.

The first place to dedicate your time is to think deeply about the role you are trying to fill and the type of person you are looking for, and to translate that into a hiring document you can discuss with a recruiter or human resources professional. At this high-level stage, focus on two areas.

First, clarify the definition of success for the role. What will this individual's mission be? What are their specific goals? What metrics will their success be measured by?

Next, identify the critical characteristics that will be necessary for a person to be effective in the role based on your definition of success. For example, is it essential they can influence without authority? Do they need to be process- and efficiency-oriented? Do they need to have strong strategic and analytical capabilities?

Don't make this an exhaustive laundry list that goes on forever and rules out just about every human being. Likewise, don't include "motherhood and apple pie" platitudes. Your list should be as specific as possible. It should be clear what is truly necessary and what is not. Focus on no more than five essentials. If a candidate doesn't possess the essentials, it should be a deal-breaker.

Apply weights to the criteria as well. The most important criteria might garner 40 percent importance, whereas the fifth on the list might be weighted 10 percent.

Next, you'll want to work with an experienced recruiter or human resources professional to translate the components on your hiring document into more actionable detail. At this stage, you'll want to begin discussing things like the approximate number of years of experience you are targeting, any essential components of the individual's background (e.g., education, certifications, time in a similar role, etc.). And you'll also discuss potential talent pools from which to source candidates. This might be a discussion about the types of roles and industries that lend themselves to fulfilling your various requirements, or school programs from which to recruit, or potential internal candidates who fit the bill.

It's likely that your organization already has a defined interview process that you will be following. If there is some flexibility to that, here are some recommendations:

If you are working with a recruiter, participate actively with the recruiter when looking through resumés. This feedback is important for the recruiter early on. Likewise, you as the hiring manager should also participate in the early phone screen process. If you and a recruiter each have a 30-minute phone conversation with several candidates and compare notes early on, it will help you align on who to pass through, and it will also help the recruiter get a better feel for who to send your way in the future. It may become less important for you to screen everybody by phone as time goes on.

When you bring a candidate in for interviews, make sure they meet with you and a few other people. Beyond about five or six people in total (including you), you tend to reach the point of diminishing returns. Some organizations operate with multiple rounds of interviews, whereas others fit everything into one day. Either way, by the time you've done all of the interviews, the candidate should have met with you (likely more than once), an HR professional, one or two members of your team, your manager, and possibly one or two other peers or superiors as appropriate. Anyone who interviews candidates should be focused on helping ensure you're bringing in an A Player who is right for the job, and they should also be helping to sell the candidate on the role and the organization.

Advice varies widely as to the effectiveness of the various interviewing techniques that exist (e.g., questions about their resumé, behavioral interviews, case questions, etc.). Through experience, I now shy away from most interview techniques and have settled on two primary approaches that we will discuss in a moment.

Many organizations also employ talent assessment tools that are designed to help you understand people's behaviors, personalities, and working styles such as the Predictive Index Behavioral Assessment® or the DiSC® personality test. While these may provide some additional data for your consideration and they can be useful in certain situations, be careful not to rely on them too heavily for hiring purposes and instead make sure you assess individuals through the approaches we will discuss below.

In my experience, Approach 2 provides the most beneficial source of insight during an interview process, but because it isn't possible to execute it under all circumstances, we will begin with the more broadly applicable of the two approaches.

Interviewing Approach 1

One of the stronger predictors of success in a future role is demonstrated success in previous roles. Strong talent tends to succeed no matter where they are placed. Approach 1 centers on trying to discern past success by digging into past experiences to the best of your abilities through interviews and extensive reference checks. While you won't necessarily be able to influence your peers and superiors to follow this approach when interviewing your candidates, I recommend that you apply the following technique:

Step through the individual's prior experiences. For each role, ask them what they were hired to do and how success was measured. Ask them whether or not they succeeded based on those metrics. Dig into where they were or were not successful and the reasons why. Ask them what other people would say about their performance during that time (including what their manager did say in performance reviews, as well as the perspectives of their peers and direct reports). Ask them what they were most proud of during their time there, what they would have done differently, and the reasons why. Then follow up with thorough reference checks and ask a similar line of questions.

It's simple and straightforward, and it tends to work better than asking behavioral questions like, "Tell me about a time when...," which allows an interviewee to answer questions they anticipated in advance with well-rehearsed stories. It also gives you a chance to dig into every role and discuss the good, the bad, and the ugly, even if a person would not otherwise choose to discuss a given experience in their past.

Interviewing Approach 2

My second recommended approach can be done in conjunction with Approach 1 and any other techniques. But as I mentioned, it's not always possible to execute this one. It depends on the role in question. But if you can employ this method, trust me when I tell you it's a game-changer.

Here is the essence of the approach:

Incorporate into the interview process a way for the candidate to execute a small task or mini-project that is representative of the type of work they would be doing in the role for which you are considering them.

As an example, when hiring for strategy and corporate development roles, I gave candidates a real-world business problem a few days in advance of in-person interviews. This was usually an actual question we faced as a business in recent history. Then I would ask them to come to the in-person interviews with a short presentation laying out their assessment of potential paths forward and a recommendation. On the interview day itself, I would invite a few people to sit in for an hour as the candidate walked through the presentation they had prepared. The candidate would also field questions from the group.

This process gave me more insight into the strength of the candidate than all of the other aspects of the interview process combined. In the case of this particular example, a significant part of the person's job was going to be thinking through big strategic problems, translating them into recommendations in presentation format, and then facilitating meetings and discussions with people to drive consensus.

So instead of asking them to talk about a time in their past when they did something similar and reflect on how well they accomplished the goal, we actually got to see firsthand how effective they were at putting together a presentation, creating a story flow, supporting an argument with logic, making presentation slides, delivering a verbal presentation, fielding questions from an audience, and many other things as well.

Over the years, some managers I have coached have pushed back on my suggestion to do this with a question like, "But what if the person cheats and gets help from somebody?"

My response to that is threefold.

First, it's unlikely that in a period of two or three days a person can fully outsource work like this unless they have an incredible network or some really good friends. (How likely would you be to spend six hours doing something on behalf of one of your friends for their job interview?)

Second, if they're savvy enough to go seek out support externally, great. I wish people who worked for me would do that more often. Why not seek out experts to help you hone your thinking and your work?

Third, how is external support during an interview markedly different from a person telling you about a time they accomplished some significant outcome in a prior role, when in fact it was a team effort, or they had meaningful support from a superior along the way? In other words, yes, there is some risk of getting an inaccurate read, at least on certain aspects of the work you are having them do. But there is risk in getting an inaccurate read through other interviewing approaches too. And based on my experience, the benefits of this approach far outweigh such a risk.

So, I encourage you to give it a try and architect a way to observe a person performing relevant work in real time. I believe it to be a more honest predictor of how they would do in the job than asking them to talk about a time they have done something similar or asking them how they would theoretically approach a situation in the future. At the very least, it will give you data and color that you otherwise wouldn't have been able to gather, and it will support you in making a great hiring decision.

Promotions and incentives

When is it time to promote an employee? Some people and organizations favor elevating people quickly and stretching them. Others wait until someone is essentially doing the job already before recognizing it with a promotion.

Strictly speaking, there isn't a right or wrong philosophy between early promotions and a more cautious approach. I favor stretching people since it's one of the best ways for them to quickly climb the learning curve. It also helps to motivate employees, whereas waiting until the point where an employee feels a promotion is overdue can be demotivating.

But what primarily dictates a person's readiness to be promoted is whether or not they have met the criteria you have established for what the next-level role requires.

The challenge is that many people and many organizations are incredibly sloppy when it comes to establishing clear criteria for career progression. An employee will ask, "What do I need to do to get to the next level?" only to find out that this hasn't been mapped out and there isn't a clear answer for them. This is a frustrating situation for any employee, and it's particularly problematic with respect to top performers who tend to be focused on doing what it takes to get to the next level.

For this reason, I urge you to take the time to map out the responsibilities and required skills and competencies for the various roles/levels you have on your team. Spell out the key characteristics that distinguish one role from the next in as much specificity as you can.

For example, suppose a "specialist" on your team is expected to provide task-level support on a project, whereas a "senior specialist" needs to be able to independently manage projects with limited oversight from you. If you are able to communicate this in an objective way, and ideally support it with examples of what task-level support looks like versus independent project management, employees will be much clearer about what they need to demonstrate before they are ready for a promotion.

Giving a promotion is usually one of the most enjoyable parts of a manager's job. It's exciting to reward an employee for their effort and performance, and it can be satisfying to deliver a piece of good news. With that being said, any time you promote somebody on your team, you run the risk of that promotion causing a negative reaction from somebody else on your team or elsewhere in the organization. The inherent question they are asking is, "Why not me?"

It may be obvious to you that the person who is not being promoted simply isn't performing at the level of the recently promoted employee. But not everyone has an accurate picture of their own performance, let alone the performance of their peers. If you have taken the time to clearly lay out criteria and requirements for each role and level on your team and you have shared this openly with your teammates, this situation arises less frequently and it is easier to work through when it does come up. Of course, there will always be some degree of subjectivity when it comes to promotion decisions. But the goal is to make a subjective process as objective as possible.

Promotions and titles are important to employees. People want to be recognized. They also want to see that they are progressing in their career. So, it's important to stay on top of this aspect of your team members' growth and ensure you're helping articulate clearly how they can continue progressing.

Compensation is the other sensitive and important topic for employees. Most organizations have guidelines and systems for how to determine employee pay and what kind of increase a specific promotion warrants. Given the differences you see across organizations and the wide variety of specific circumstances, it would be difficult to provide any concrete guidance on matters of compensation.

Instead, let's focus on when it makes sense to increase somebody's pay.

In addition to doing so in conjunction with a promotion, you should also adjust somebody's pay any time they take on a meaningful set of new responsibilities, even if they aren't being promoted to a new level. Not every manager/organization follows this guidance (and there are certainly exceptions to this suggestion), but asking somebody to do more because of "the visibility" or "the learning opportunity" it will afford them without compensating them can eventually backfire and cause employee frustration and degradation of morale. It is okay to do this occasionally, but be wary of creating a situation where an employee may feel the organization is taking advantage of their good will.

Another time to increase somebody's pay is when you come to the realization that an employee is underpaid relative to their market value. Larger organizations often invest in research and consulting services, so they have market data with which to benchmark employee pay for similar positions. They then set pay ranges for roles based on where they want to be relative to industry ranges. If that data isn't available to you through your company, you can often do your own research by searching for equivalent roles on Glassdoor or through other online sources. The reason it's important to ensure a position is marked to market is that you don't want to be caught in a situation where employees recognize they are underpaid and leave you.

Some organizations make it a practice to adjust employee salaries with inflation as part of an annual performance review process, but this is not ubiquitous.

The final situation to comment on is when an employee asks for (or demands) a pay increase. I discourage you from adjusting somebody's pay under that circumstance unless you recognize that they truly are underpaid relative to their value. Otherwise, you can create headaches for yourself by giving into demands. It often creates a cascade of effects such as inequity across your team. Even in a situation where an employee is threatening to leave and asks you to counter or match an offer they have at another job, usually giving them a pay increase will only temporarily prevent them from leaving. Anyone who has gotten to the point where they are actively pursuing other opportunities usually has one foot out the door and tends not to stick around for long. The best way to deal with a situation where an employee asks for a pay increase is to establish a development plan with concrete goals and tie the pay increase to the employee meeting those goals.

Terminating

Most people with management and leadership experience will tell you that the hardest part of the job is having to let people go. This has been true in my experience as well.

But great leaders will tell you that one of the biggest mistakes made by leaders and managers is waiting too long to take action when a performance issue arises. It's understandable that this happens—most people want to give somebody as much time as possible to turn things around. But what often happens is that the desire to give a person ample time to correct things turns into a situation where you draw things out beyond the point at which it's clear that the desired turnaround isn't going to happen. Retired Brunswick CEO Mark Schwabero says, "When you have a known personnel problem, if you do not nip it in the bud, it will come back to haunt you, I promise."

During the period you are waiting for the employee to turn things around, the bad situation usually gets worse. It drags out the emotionally taxing aspects of the issue for you and for the individual. It leads directly to lost productivity. And even though we tend to think we are doing a service for the individual in question, often this isn't the case. It is an uncomfortable and sometimes painful situation to be struggling to perform in the eyes of your superiors and to know your job is at risk. (Most people can tell they are on shaky ground, even if you haven't confronted the issue directly yet). If a person isn't excelling, it is usually the case that their skills and aptitudes are not a good fit for that particular role or organization. Given time, they will likely land in something that's well-suited to them and they will be much happier and more successful.

Furthermore, keeping underperforming talent around can have a negative impact on other people on your team, and especially on top performers. It sends a message to your team that you do not want to be sending. Some may see you as a weak manager. Others may see it as a sign that mediocrity is acceptable on your team, which could translate into team members reducing their effort level. And still others may become frustrated that they are carrying so much of the load while the underperformers fail to pull their weight, which can turn into negative feelings directed toward you for not resolving the performance issue.

As challenging as it is, knowing when to cut the ties with an underperforming employee is an essential skill of a mature manager.

It's important to note that when you find yourself at the point where you know it is time to part ways with an employee, this should not be the first time the employee is hearing about issues with their performance. If it is, you haven't been doing your job coaching and providing feedback along the way. Most employees who are being terminated due to performance issues should see the writing on the wall, and you are the one putting that writing on the wall for them. (There are exceptions to this, such as an ethics violation that results in a quick and decisive termination, or a round of layoffs where employee performance is not the primary cause of separation from the company.)

The decision to terminate has legal implications, so it's critical that you work with a human resources professional to follow the appropriate processes. Legal requirements also vary based on geography, which is another reason to follow guidance from human resources.

Prior to formalizing a decision to terminate, it is likely you will be putting the employee on a Performance Improvement Plan (PIP) for a period of time to give them an opportunity to turn around their performance. PIPs are formally documented processes whereby you communicate to an employee their underperformance, the specific improvements you and the organization need to see and over what time frame, and the consequence for their not demonstrating the required improvement (i.e., termination). The time frame for a PIP process to unfold is often two to three months, making it that much more important for you to move quickly when you spot performance issues and initiate a PIP process. It is likely that your Human Resources department has their own version of a PIP that you should be using, but please see the appendix for an example PIP. The example PIP demonstrates the level of detail needed to correctly set the employee up for success, as well as to protect yourself and the company if they are unable to succeed.

When you've made a final decision to terminate and it comes time to communicate that decision to the individual, take time to prepare for the discussion. If this is the first time you have terminated an employee, work with a human resources professional to create an outline or script for the discussion. It goes without saying that you want to deliver the news in as respectful a way as possible. If you've never lost your job, it's difficult to understand what that person may experience. Even if you have, every person and every situation is unique. If the person becomes emotional, try to stay as dispassionate and unemotional as you can, while still maintaining the kindness and respect that the person deserves. But don't improvise—stick to your chosen language and talking points for legal reasons as well as for reasons of ensuring the best outcome during the interaction. That is the reason for doing the preparation in the first place.

When it is time to share the news, make sure you've carved out ample time to address your team after the fact. Prepare talking points for them as well, and work with human resources since there will be guidelines as to what you can/cannot or should/should not say. Of course, it's best to be as transparent as possible, but this is one of those situations where legality and respect for the other person may trump the level of transparency you might otherwise prefer.

It's also good practice to sit down with each team member individually after the news becomes public to make sure they are doing okay and to understand their concerns. Even in situations where you might think a person's performance shortfalls were obvious to everybody, they often are not obvious to every one of the terminated employee's peers. That means some people could view the termination as an indication that they may also be at risk of losing their jobs. Or if they were close to the individual and believe that the individual was an asset to the team, they may view the termination as a bad decision and assign negative feelings about it to you or to the broader organization. While you may not be able to respond to all of these situations in a direct way, address them to the best of your ability. And continue to treat the terminated individual with respect in all of your interactions with others.

Terminating people will not be something you want to do; it will only ever be something you feel you have to do because it's the right thing to do in the situation. All you can do is make the best of an unfortunate situation, acting with integrity throughout and keeping everyone's best interests in mind as you progress through the process.

Accepting resignations

Sometimes it won't be you having to let somebody go, but you'll lose somebody on your team because they decide it's time for them to move on. It's all part of managing a team.

When somebody resigns, don't take it personally. It usually isn't about you. There are a lot of factors that lead somebody to make the decision to leave.

You may think it's important to dig in to understand why they are leaving when they present the news to you. It's common to reason that you may be able to give them a counteroffer and "save them," or you may simply learn some important feedback that can shape how you and the broader organization operate.

But unless you have a uniquely close working relationship with that person, avoid that temptation in the moment. Likewise, don't dig for other details such where they are going next. It is fine to discuss it if they volunteer any of that information, but it's not your place to ask that in the moment since it places them in an uncomfortable position. It's best to accept their resignation gracefully and allow a more neutral person, such as a human resources professional, to determine if there might be an opportunity to save that person or to gather feedback on you, the team, and the organization through an exit interview.

Every situation is unique, so you'll want to work with a human resources professional to agree on when and how to communicate that person's news more broadly. Usually, the individual will want to personally share the news with some co-workers. But beyond that, you may be the one communicating the news to the rest of your team.

Many managers are uncertain about how to socialize this news with their team. Before you are even ready to socialize, you need to build the transition plan, including who that person's direct reports will report into on an interim basis, how the individual's workload will be handled now and in the future, whether or not the role will be backfilled and by when, and so on. It's ideal if you can involve the person who is leaving in that process and pull affected people in as appropriate to come up with a robust plan.

The transition plan usually dictates who on the team you need to communicate with first and how you need to approach them. Once the people who are directly impacted by the transition have been informed of the change, there will likely be others you need to share the news with as well.

In any of these interactions, keep the message positive — let the person/people you're communicating with know that the individual has decided to move on, express your gratitude for their contributions, and wish them well in their next endeavor. This is true even in the rare case that the resignation is reflective of deeper morale issues that you are concerned may lead to further churn on your team. People will be looking to your reaction to gauge the situation, so calm positivity is best. If the person/people who are hearing the news were not involved in transition planning, this is also the time to lay out the components of the transition plan. Finally, if you plan to have a farewell gathering, mention that as well, as it is another way to keep things as upbeat as possible.

Unless the resignation is "un-regrettable," it can be difficult news to receive, especially if this is not yet something you've had to cope with as a manager. But we all have to do what's best for ourselves in our professional careers, so try to be understanding and keep the big picture in mind. And remember that as challenging as it may make things in the short term, every vacancy creates an opportunity for you to bring in fresh, outstanding talent and to make other changes to how you and your team operate. So, make the best of it!

In summary

The skills involved in building an A Team are by no means easy to master. Even the greatest leaders will tell you that they have plenty of scars from poor hiring and talent-related decisions. Every manager does. It just isn't possible to be flawless. Everyone makes mistakes.

But taking the time to grow and develop your own capabilities in this area can lead to massive step-changes in the profile and quality of your team. The more time you spend in management roles, the more you will come to see firsthand how powerful a lever it is that you have in your hands—one that only grows in importance as you take on larger roles and greater responsibility in the future.

Chapter 10:

Managing Remote/Distributed Teams

It's likely that at some point in your career, if you haven't already, you will be managing a team that includes individuals in other locations. Historically, this has been referred to as managing "remote" teams, but more recently this term has been replaced by the term "distributed."

The trend toward distributed workforces has been on the rise for many years, but the circumstances surrounding the COVID-19 pandemic accelerated this shift for many organizations. It's very likely this trend will continue as more organizations recognize some of the benefits of moving to an increasingly distributed model, including reduced overhead and the ability to access a global talent pool.

Whether you are managing in an in-person model, a distributed model, or a hybrid of the two, the fundamentals of strong management remain consistent. It's still about cultivating trust and performance. It's still critical to embody the seven essential characteristics of great managers. You will still be setting goals, prioritizing and delegating work, coaching and providing feedback, and motivating and inspiring your team.

But there are some important differences between managing co-located teams and managing distributed teams, so let's discuss these differences and how best to work with your team in light of them.

The first thing a manager has to do when leading a distributed team is let go of any antiquated views regarding measuring an employee's effectiveness, value, or commitment based on face time, and instead learn to gauge an employee's success purely based on their output and tangible contributions.

This tends to be one of the biggest management gaps that is revealed as organizations undergo a shift from an office-based culture to a distributed model. All too often, organizations and managers have placed too much emphasis on face time, which turns out to be a very weak proxy for what truly matters—the degree to which an employee successfully achieves the objectives of their role.

Not only that, but some organizations and managers make matters worse by spending time and resources on oversight measures, such as tracking how many hours an employee is working based on how much they are signed on. These Big Brother efforts are almost always a waste of time and often backfire by reducing the felt sense of trust and autonomy the organization or manager is placing in that individual.

It is a far better use of your time to focus on employing the methods discussed in this book around establishing very clear goals, objectives and expectations for your team. Then you can measure an employee's contributions directly.

With that as the foundation, the next area to focus on is to make sure you have the right tools and work processes in place. As a baseline, the right tools include all necessary hardware and software for an individual to perform their role from anywhere, access to any digital collaboration tools your team uses (e.g., Slack), as well as video and audio-conferencing capabilities. You'll also want to make sure one of the tools allows for quick and easy screen sharing.

With these in place, the next area to focus on is establishing expectations and norms for how you operate and train your team on your work processes and tools, just as you would if you were managing an in-person team.

When I manage distributed teams, I like to provide rules of thumb for when we use video, audio, digital collaboration tools, email, text and so forth. As we've discussed earlier, generally there's an optimal tool for a given circumstance.

For example, for performance reviews and formal feedback chats that can't be accomplished in person, I always use video except when it isn't possible due to extenuating circumstances. Video is the most formal medium and it's as close as you can get to an in-person chat. I also recommend that my team use video for important meetings requiring a high degree of engagement.

But if we need to hop on a quick unscheduled one-on-one or group call, I ask my teams to use audio. Sometimes we need to use our video-conferencing tool for screen sharing purposes, but everyone knows that it's perfectly fine to have their video turned off under that circumstance. The reason for this is that I've found it's important to give people the courtesy of choosing whether they are prepared to be on video on short notice (e.g., they may have concerns about how they look) and I don't want any norms that deter people from quickly convening and collaborating.

My teams have also established other norms and tricks, such as having someone type up notes during our team meetings in a document or notes app that everyone has access to in real time so we can all track them and keep a check on our shared understanding of meeting outcomes and decisions.

I share these ideas with you not to say that this is the right way, but to illustrate the sorts of things you'll want to make explicit if you manage distributed teams.

With the right processes and tools in place, coupled with explicit norms and expectations for how you operate as a distributed team, the next area to address is compensating for some of the inherent weaknesses of a distributed model.

To begin with, when you are a manager of an in-person team, a portion of how you keep a pulse on how things are going takes place informally, often simply by walking around. You get looped in through quick hallway chats. You can tell how somebody on your team is feeling by watching their body language as they walk in in the morning and you can spot certain issues with relative ease.

Without the ability to manage by walking around, it's that much more important to make sure you're having frequent check-ins with teammates. One-on-ones with your team are that much more of an imperative in a distributed model.

Similarly, much of the relationship-building that happens at work takes place in the hallway or the kitchen or at the beginning or end of meetings as people are congregating or dispersing. Without these informal touchpoints, work can shift too far in the direction of being "all business all the time." This is something to be conscious of not just between you and your teammates, but also between your teammates.

It's important to build in ways to compensate for this gap. One way my teams have done this is to open up all of our team meetings with five minutes of scheduled time for informal chatting. Sometimes we will task somebody in the meeting with coming up with an interesting or provocative non-work-related question to ask the group at the start of a meeting, and then take turns having each person answer. It may seem forced to approach it in this way, but in my experience it's necessary to do things like this or work loses an important human element.

The other big challenge inherent in a distributed model that I have observed (although this one is also a strength when viewed through other lenses) is that much more of your team's work tends to shift toward written communication.

A couple of the reasons this happens is because, as you embrace the ideology of focusing on people's output as opposed to face time (including virtual face time), you naturally shift toward providing your team greater autonomy to get their work done in the way that best suits them (e.g., a night owl who does their best work after 7 p.m. has the flexibility to do that). You also tend to naturally gravitate toward doing more work independently except when it's appropriate and necessary to work together. (This is another inherent strength of the distributed model, because in my experience, office-based cultures rely too heavily on meetings to move forward things that don't truly require meetings.) With more of your team's work being spread out across different hours of the day, there is a greater need to rely on digital collaboration tools and email—written forms of communication—to account for people plugging in at different times. It's also worth mentioning that the larger and more spread out across time zones your team is, the further things are pushed in this direction.

With a greater reliance on written communication, it's important to look out for some of the potential pitfalls.

First, people have the tendency in this model to default first to written communication, when often it is simply faster or more effective to hop on a quick call or video chat. Continue to impress upon your team the importance of leaning on the right medium for the task at hand.

Second, a greater reliance on written communication places a high burden on a person's quality of writing. Thus, writing quality becomes a crucial skill to screen for in interviews. It's also something to train and provide consistent coaching on. Everyone on your team needs to elevate the clarity of their written communications. Emails need to contain necessary context while also striving for an appropriate level of succinctness, without room for erroneous interpretation, so the recipient can respond or take action without the need to double back. We have all received an email that could easily be read two different ways by two different people. When a big portion of your team's output happens through written modalities, these issues become particularly costly in terms of both efficiency and effectiveness.

Lastly, it's so crucial to make sure everyone understands the importance of tone in written communication. All too often, a person's writing comes across as too abrupt and creates unnecessary tension in a collaborative environment. Coach people on how mission-critical it is to write with a friendly tone. Teach people to include pleasantries. Don't be afraid to include emojis—it might seem odd in a professional setting, but it's a simple way to communicate friendliness when words might be too fraught with the potential for misinterpretation.

Likewise, it's important to stress to your team the need to give people the benefit of the doubt. As sensitive as a person can be in crafting a paragraph with the right tone, almost anything can be interpreted in a way that is other than what the writer intended to convey. It's much more common that the reason behind a terse email is something benign, like the person was rushed, rather than something loaded, like the person was feeling hostility toward the recipient. Teach your team to assume the best of intentions—a principle that applies in spades to written communication, but extends to many other areas of collaboration as well.

Giving people the benefit of the doubt is particularly important to keep in mind if you are a distributed team in a largely office-based organization where you need to collaborate frequently with other groups and functions. Be patient with those other groups and functions. If they aren't used to working in a distributed model, it's likely there will be some clumsiness in collaborating with them. Your workflow, processes, and norms are likely very different from theirs, and most of the awkwardness can be explained by that rather than by the assumed intentions of the people in the other group.

At this point, we've discussed the most important ingredients for successfully managing a distributed team. Focus on outcomes. Put into place the right tools and processes. Couple this with norms and expectations that allow you to extract the most out of working in a distributed model. Acknowledge and proactively compensate for the inherent gaps in distributed work environments. Encourage people to approach collaboration with a benevolent mindset, especially with respect to written communication.

Before leaving this topic, there is one final point to make: A distributed model isn't inherently better or worse than an in-person model. Both have strengths and weaknesses. I'm also of the opinion that if done well, a good portion of knowledge work is better suited for distributed (or largely distributed) models.

But there is no substitute for carving out time to get together in person. Even if you have a global team and you're only able to do it sporadically, spending a few weeks together—or even just one week a year—can go an incredibly long way in cultivating and solidifying positive working relationships between your team members. No amount of video chats will ever match spending time in a room with each other, going out to dinner and sharing stories about life outside of work, and spending time shoulder-to-shoulder as you work toward a mutual objective. Embrace the distributed model, but supplement with the necessary in-person time to make it a true success on all dimensions.

Chapter 11:

Unexpected Challenges That New Managers Face

In the opening of this book, I shared with you that becoming a manager is one of the biggest (if not *the biggest*) transitions you can go through in your professional career. But until you've gone through it, it can be hard to imagine exactly why that could be the case.

Many people have assumptions about what it must be like to be a manager. But the reality is often very different from what one would expect, on both a practical and an emotional level. In this chapter, we'll explore some of the things you tend not to hear about. We'll reveal what it is actually like being a manager as we unpack some of the unexpected challenges you may face in this role. While everybody's situation is different and it's possible you may not experience every issue, there is a good chance you'll have to overcome most of these challenges at some point in your managerial career. They aren't reserved for new managers only.

So, if you are new to management or haven't made the transition yet, then hopefully going into these situations with eyes wide open will make your life a little easier. And if you already have a good amount of management experience, this may normalize some of what you have experienced (or are experiencing), and it may also highlight some things to be on the lookout for as you take on expanded roles in the future.

Authority

It's common to think that when you step into a managerial role, people's behavior toward you will instantly and automatically line up with your newly granted authority. But this isn't always the case. Some people may treat you as an authority, but other people will not. This can be a bit of a rude awakening to some new managers. Some managers even feel like they are not respected, such as when a certain team member appears to treat you differently than they have treated other managers.

It's helpful to remember that respect is something that is earned; it doesn't automatically come with a new role or title. Just because you are somebody's manager, it doesn't mean they will look at you and treat you the same as they have treated their other managers, right out of the gates. There is a good chance you will have to cultivate the right dynamics with people over time through your words and actions. That's actually a good thing, even if it doesn't feel like it is at first. It pushes you to step up your game as a leader.

Even in the rare example where a brazen employee treats you in such a way that you think, *Do they realize I'm going to be the one writing their performance review and making compensation decisions for them?*, you still don't want to have to lean on the authority that's been given to you unless you absolutely need to do so. Resorting to leading by authority that you have been granted is almost always the weaker move. Influencing people through the level of command you *earn* is the mark of a truly great manager and leader.

So, don't be surprised if the instant change to your role does not translate to instant feelings of authority. Work to gain the respect and loyalty of your new team members and peers through how you carry yourself, your demonstration of the essential characteristics of great managers, and by employing the skills we have discussed throughout the book.

Imposter syndrome

It's incredibly common to suffer from "imposter syndrome" when you step into a new role. If you've never experienced it, imposter syndrome is just as it sounds—you feel like an imposter. Sometimes you have the feeling that your recent promotion and people's perception of your skills and abilities aren't deserved or warranted. You feel overrated. You may feel like it's only a matter of time before you are discovered for being a fraud—that the shoe will drop and somebody will realize you don't actually have the skills and capabilities needed to do your job.

Imposter syndrome can happen to anyone who takes on a new role that is out of their comfort zone. But often it's more acutely felt by people in managerial ranks. There are more eyeballs on managers. They have direct reports who are watching them closely. It can all feel quite intense.

Something that can add to the intensity and make you feel as though you *actually are* a real imposter is that you may in fact *know for certain* that you are less knowledgeable or experienced than certain team members you are managing. Perhaps you have adopted responsibility over some roles that you yourself have never been in or roles that you know little about. Perhaps you have taken on a direct report who is much older than you or one who has many more years of relevant work experience. In such situations, the imposter feeling might seem like a fact. You might think to yourself, *I am not qualified to do this job and somehow the people who gave it to me don't realize that yet.* It might not be possible for you to recognize that this is an irrational fear.

This can become increasingly common the higher you rise in an organization. The higher you go, the larger the jobs and responsibilities will be, and the bigger the jumps in responsibility will feel. Also, practically speaking, the teams and organizations underneath you get bigger, making it even less likely you will have a thorough understanding of how everyone's job beneath you is done.

But that's not your job.

Great managers don't need to know how to do every team member's job better than those people to be highly effective as a manager. Great managers are in a role that serves an entirely different purpose—they lead people. It's also worth mentioning that oftentimes, managers who know how to do everyone's job better than everyone else suffer from a significant weakness—they think they know it all and try to control things too much.

When you step into any role for the first time, you probably do have a ton to learn. But that doesn't make you an imposter. You've simply been pushed back down to the beginner end of the competence spectrum. And the feeling of being an imposter is almost always unwarranted; it's just a period of low confidence.

Nonetheless, it's a natural sentiment felt by most people. You're by no means alone. It can *feel* like you're the only person who has ever felt this way because most people hide this feeling. The chances are high that there are people beside you and above you who are feeling that way right now. But guess what? Most of them wouldn't dare talk about it, because in their minds that would be confirming to other people what they've been fearing—that the truth of their incompetence will be discovered.

The best way to deal with a case of imposter syndrome is to recognize what you're dealing with—it's an irrational fear resulting from a temporary period of overwhelm. Be kind to yourself. And most importantly, focus on adding value in the ways you uniquely can using the strengths you bring to the table during the early days when you're giving yourself time to learn the things you don't know.

Don't feel as though you have to hide your weaknesses or gaps in knowledge either, which tends to exacerbate imposter syndrome. If you take the approach of genuinely trying to support your team members with what you have to offer and displaying humility, they will reciprocate by teaching you what you need to know to be effective in your new role. If you demonstrate the essential characteristics of great managers, they will respect you and will genuinely want to help you succeed. Look out for them and they will look out for you.

And remember that the fact that you can't do somebody's job can be a reason for them to feel good. If they see that you need them and that you recognize this by showing them you value them, you will foster trust and loyalty between each other and will boost their morale.

Most of all, remember that imposter syndrome will fade in time. You will get comfortable in your role. You will gain confidence. It just takes time.

Changes to work relationships

When you are elevated to a new role in the management ranks, you're now at a different level in the organization, and your peer group literally changes overnight. Because of this, you simply can't act the same way you used to with colleagues who were previously your peers. Many people are unprepared for this degree of change.

As an example, you may have had colleagues you previously would have vented with about certain subjects behind closed doors, but doing so now would no longer be appropriate. But your former peers won't want to see your relationship dynamic change. They may treat you the same way they did before your promotion and you may feel tugged at to do the same.

As tempting as that may be, it's best to simply act in accordance with your new role no matter the situation. Yes, relationships dynamics will change. It's possible you'll no longer act like buddies with somebody who used to be your peer. But that's all part of what you sign up for when you take a role like this.

Sometimes, this sort of situation can be exacerbated by how you were promoted. Sometimes, new managers to have to manage someone who was once their peer. That former peer may or may not deal with your promotion in a productive way. Occasionally, that person actually wanted the job you just snagged and they are feeling picked over. They might not be cheering you on.

That's all okay. Again, it's part of what you signed up for, but more importantly, it tends to fade over time as people acclimate to the new situation. That's especially true if you treat people respectfully, look out for them, and embody the essential characteristics of great managers.

It's also good in any change to shift your focus away from what you're losing to what you're gaining. You now have a new peer group to get to know. True, the dynamics may be changing with a former peer in a way you'd rather not have to see it change, but chances are there's something great waiting in the wings with your new peer group.

Second-order effects of your decisions

As a manager, you quickly find you are making more decisions than you ever had to before. Even if you're the best of the best when it comes to empowering your employees and boosting their autonomy, you will still be amazed at how often you're having to make decisions.

Decision-making itself is a competency you will want to hone. But one of the hardest lessons new managers learn has to do with the ripple effects of their decisions. Any time you make a decision, it is likely to have many implications and knock-on effects that you weren't expecting.

Here is a simple example. Employee A comes to you and tells you they've been offered a position at another company and unless you match that salary and give them a title bump, they are going to leave. You weigh your options and decide that the employee is too important to let go of at this time, so you give them a salary and title increase. The employee agrees to stay. You are grateful for having solved your problem.

But after others learn about Employee A's new title, you hear that Employees B and C are now unhappy. Your decision, which may have temporarily resolved your first problem, has now created two new problems in its place.

When you're a manager, not only are you going to be making more decisions, but because you have a greater scope of responsibility, the downstream implications of your decisions tend to reach further as well. It takes time and experience to get better at adopting a wider lens and thinking through all of the potential implications of a decision. And taking time to think through decisions needs to be balanced by speed of decision-making—a vital characteristic of nimble teams and organizations. Great managers are measured but decisive.

If you're new to this, all you can do is do your best. There is no substitute for time in role and more at-bats in making decisions of all types. The reality is that you need to make enough decisions and directly observe the types of unexpected things that manifest as a consequence of your decisions before you have enough data you can apply to improving how you make decisions. Be patient with yourself. Also remember that great managers do not make decisions in a vacuum. Involve your team in decision-making. Test your thinking (and your team's thinking) with your peers, your manager, or a mentor to increase your odds of making a good decision in a tough situation.

Underestimating what you got yourself into

When I took my first job out of school, I was convinced I was at the hardest stage of my career. I was the lowest person on the totem pole. I was given all the grunt work and was frequently overworked as well. I had little control over my work life since it was all dictated by the people above me.

I became convinced that, if I could only get promoted and become a manager, things would get easier. After all, I would have leverage. Other people would be doing the work I was doing. I would be the one telling everyone what I wanted them to do while I got to do the more interesting and important things.

Not only that, but I believed things would get even better the higher I went in an organization. I envisioned the senior levels as being the cushiest of jobs, where I'd finally get to coast because I'd worked my way up to that level and earned the right to sit back. The pace of work would slow down, my life would be more relaxed, and I'd be happy because I had "arrived."

Wrong! It's humorous now to think of how naïve that was. That progression may be true in certain professions, but it wasn't the case for mine. Yes, some earlier challenges did go away. Yes, my autonomy did grow. But in my experience, every new level I reached brought bigger challenges than I ever could have expected. My workload wasn't less than before—it was more. The work itself was usually harder, or it was equally difficult but in different ways. The pressure tended to rise with each new level I reached. In my experience, my initial assumption wasn't just a little bit wrong—I had it completely backwards.

If you find yourself in a management role wondering how you could have possibly underestimated the challenge as much as you did, you would not be the first nor will you be the last. It is a tremendous responsibility to be in charge of other people. Managers often spend most of their day with their team members, handling the demands that come up, only to realize they have no more time in the workday to do the work they have on their own plates. They end up staying late or catching up on that work in the evenings and on the weekends, only to have the cycle repeat again and again.

Bigger roles also tend to correspond with more pressure because of the optics of a higher-profile job. Everyone's job is about problem solving at the most fundamental level. When you rise a level in the hierarchy, now you are responsible for working through all of the biggest problems that bubble up from within your span of control. The things that the people beneath you couldn't handle on their own hit your desk. By definition, those problems will be a lot bigger than the ones you faced before. This principle follows you all the way up the chain, with the size and impact of problems growing larger at each new level of organizational hierarchy.

Also, when you're in charge of teams and organizations, you now have personnel-related challenges to deal with, which are sometimes the trickiest types of problems you will see. Whether it's a performance challenge, an unhappy employee threatening to move on, an interpersonal conflict, an ethics violation, or any of the countless other possible scenarios, all of these people-related challenges require time and attention. Resolving them usually doesn't leave you feeling like you advanced the ball toward your objectives. Often, they are time-consuming issues that you need to address just to keep the ship afloat.

Because of all of this, one of the most common emotions people feel when taking on a management role for the first time is overwhelm. It's hard work. You feel pressure to succeed. You are learning a new role, but on top of that, you are learning to be a manager. It's a double whammy.

But if you find that you feel this way, you're in good company. Lots of people feel this way. It will get better. One of the best things you can do is keep calm, build your systems for how you operate so you effectively manage your time, learn the art of delegation, learn how to let go of control, and focus as much time as you can on building up your team since that's the greatest source of leverage and return on investment of your time.

Make time for family

If you are going through this transition and have a significant other, a budding family, or you have several children already, make sure that you make the time for them, too. As we have discussed several times, this is one of the biggest transitions that you will go through in your professional life, and it takes extra time out of your day. I would estimate that for several months after being promoted (or longer), many people will be working an additional 10 or 20 percent more hours per week learning how to manage, falling down, picking themselves up, and doing it again until they get into a rhythm.

Your biggest supporters are your loved ones. Please do not forget to make time for them just because you are stretched at work. They will be with you for a long time, and in many ways, they are the unsung heroes who are enabling your career success.

Also, remember that they can be invaluable as unbiased sounding boards when talking through issues you face at work because they know you best. Include them—they will appreciate it, and you might learn something about them and about yourself as well.

Stay positive

If you haven't experienced these challenges, you might be coming away from this section with a new level of anxiety. Keep in mind that this is just one side of the transition—the side focused on some of the difficult things people tend to face when stepping into a management role.

But all of this will only serve your growth. It will shape you in ways you could not imagine. If you are willing to stretch yourself and take on such challenges, the feeling of pride and accomplishment that awaits you will be profoundly rewarding.

Chapter 12:

Managing Through a Crisis

Over the past two decades, the world has seen three crises that have rocked the stock market, eroded a massive amount of corporate earnings, driven unemployment to unprecedented levels, and even rattled healthcare systems to the core: the dot-com bubble in the early 2000's, the Great Recession in 2009, and COVID-19 in 2020.

These crises have each created intense situations that tested managers and leaders in unexpected ways.

For instance, as COVID-19 began to spread and governments and organizations took action to implement social distancing measures, we started to see growing tension between manufacturing laborers and office-based workers. As laborers were required to continue going into the factory while office-based workers were able to protect themselves from the pandemic by working from home, laborers felt like second-class citizens.

While this chasm formed, the weaker managers continued with their usual day-to-day responsibilities and focused on trying to make the quarter while they sat at home.

However, the strong managers saw this issue forming and attacked it directly by establishing daily video calls with their teams in the plant, or by sending a rotating manager or executive into the plant every morning to spend time with the labor force. The strong managers led from the front, and they recognized that in a time of crisis, it's your people who matter the most.

The three crises mentioned above were all global issues with widespread impact. But there are lots of smaller-scale crises that arise that are confined to an industry, a sector, an organization, or even a team. When these crises arise, the same fundamentals apply—great managers lead from the front and they recognize that it's the people who matter most.

I worked for a large crane manufacturer years ago. One day, there was a tragic accident at the plant that led to multiple fatalities. To my knowledge, the CEO took the appropriate actions over the next few days including halting plant operations, triaging the situation, calling families, working with investigatory authorities, understanding the root causes, and reassuring his organization. However, a few days later, the CEO attended the Superbowl rather than being present at the funerals of the deceased. Imagine how this made the laborers, managers, and other team members feel. One can only imagine that he squandered loyalty his team may have had for him.

Any crisis, big or small, is a time when people look toward the person in charge for comfort and reassurance. Leaders and managers who remain calm, clear-headed, focused on their people, and action-oriented inspire confidence in difficult times. When they effectively navigate a crisis, strong leaders and managers come out the other side with a new level of respect and loyalty from their teams.

Weak managers are prone to panic and over-reaction during crises. They lose the hearts and minds of their teams and have difficulty recovering from it.

As Rahm Emanuel once said, "Never allow a good crisis to go to waste."

A crisis is also an important time for a strong leader to take a step back and assess the business or organization. Sometimes the crisis creates the ideal conditions to push the reset button in certain areas or to take steps to plan for the future beyond the crisis.

For instance, COVID-19 created the unusual situation of preventing sales forces that were used to traveling two or three days per week from leaving their homes. And even though sales reps were working from home, they often had several hours of open capacity per day because their clients were also slowing down.

Strong sales managers turned this into an opportunity to build new capabilities, such as having their sales reps refresh their key account plans and having them improve their sales skills through daily training programs. They were able to ensure their sales teams effectively utilized 10 hours per week of free capacity (the equivalent of about 400 hours per month across a team of 10 sales reps). Contrast that with weaker managers who let that time slip through the cracks. Never waste a good crisis.

Strong managers demonstrate six competencies when managing through a crisis. While it's important to meet a crisis head-on without hesitation, it's valuable to quickly assemble your own action plan that ensures you are demonstrating these competencies as you navigate the difficult situation:

1. *Be visible, purposeful, and authentic* and demonstrate to people that you are thinking of them, that you are in this together, and that you can be counted on to provide them with timely fact-based information.

2. *Use the principal of "commander's intent,"* a military term that describes the process of defining what a successful mission looks like from your perspective and ensuring everyone is marching forward in the same direction.

3. *Practice the pause* during this time by frequently asking how people are doing, and actively listening before providing a thoughtful response.

4. *Engage externally* to keep a pulse on what is going on around you and to gauge how stakeholders are reacting to how you and the organization are handling the situation.

5. *Cut through bureaucracy* and remove red tape whenever necessary to keep everyone empowered and action-oriented.

6. *Keep imagination and creativity alive* so that your team knows you are looking for new ways to solve problems. Imagination and creativity can also become beacons of hope during difficult times.

Revisit your plan daily and pay attention to the following principles when managing through the crisis:

- Be visible and communicative.
- Read everything you write twice before sending and pay special attention to tone to ensure communications are positive and constructive.

- Don't allow yourself to get completely swallowed up by short-term and tactical issues; try to keep everyone's head up and looking toward the future.
- Don't default to going back to old ways—use the crisis as an opportunity to reassess and chart a new course for the future.
- Most importantly, stay calm, level-headed, action-oriented, and focused on the welfare of your people.

Chapter 13:

Determining If It Is Time to Leave

O ver the years, one of the most common questions I have received from people I have managed and mentored is this:

"How do I know when it's time for me to leave the organization?"

A lot of people wrestle with knowing when it's time to move on. I would like to share my perspective about how to think through this, since you will likely find yourself asking this question at various points throughout your career. Likewise, when you are in leadership positions, others may come to you looking for mentorship advice about this topic.

This is how I have approached the question in my own career journey. To me, there are five criteria upon which to assess your job:

1. Do I enjoy the work itself?
2. Do I like the people?
3. Am I fairly/generously paid?
4. Is it meeting my professional development needs?
5. Do I have work/life balance?

I see these as the five most important dimensions when it comes to job quality and satisfaction.

I believe these are self-explanatory, but I do want to comment on the first question. "Enjoying work" can mean different things to different people. One person may enjoy that they are being intellectually challenged. Another person may love marketing and enjoy a role in that function regardless of the specific industry they are working in. Someone else may only be satisfied if they are deeply engaged with the mission of the organization. So, the essence of the first question is about how engaged you feel in your own work and/or the work of the organization as a whole.

If you can answer "yes" to all five of these criteria, you probably wouldn't even think about leaving, and for good reason. If you have all five of these in a job, you have struck gold.

Likewise, if your job checks the boxes on four of these, I would strongly encourage you to stay put. It's rare to have everything you want in any job. You're in a great situation.

If you have three out of five of these in a job, this is the point at which I recommend putting feelers out. You're not in a bad situation, but you could do better. Also, things may get better in time, but they could get worse. So, it's good to have a low-key search process going on in the background.

If your job meets two out of five of these criteria, it's time to aggressively pursue your alternatives.

If you have one out of five (or zero), what are you waiting for? You should have left months ago!

Although these are framed as yes/no questions, there is a spectrum of possibilities along each dimension. For example, your answer may be an emphatic "no" on two of them and a weak "yes" on the other three. You'll want to factor that into your thought process.

Also, certain criteria will be more important to you than others, so factor that into your thought process too.

The importance you assign to each of these factors will naturally fluctuate throughout your life as well. For example, I was more concerned about work/life balance after I had a child than I was before that point. So, it's useful to revisit these questions periodically over time.

Likewise, the degree to which your job meets these criteria will fluctuate over time. Roles change, leadership changes, ownership changes, market conditions change — things rarely stay put for too long. Often, if things slip below a threshold of acceptability, you'll have to ask yourself, "Is this the new norm?" You won't always know. You'll have to trust your gut.

Of course, all of this is general guidance — take it with a grain of salt and make it your own. I have used this effectively over the course of my own career, assessing my situation every few months and making changes when I see that things have fallen below a certain level. I have found the framework to be a useful way to approach an otherwise complex question, and I hope it's helpful to you and to those you mentor.

Chapter 14:

Parting Advice on Your

Journey to Greatness

We have come a long way. We delved deeply into the qualities great managers embody. We talked through the keys to translating your vision, strategy, and objectives into goals for your team. We highlighted the criticality of delegation and how to go about it in the most effective way possible. We examined the qualities of a strong coach and the techniques for engaging in productive feedback discussions and performance reviews. We explored the ways in which you can adjust and optimize your managerial approach to align with a particular situation and employee. We dove into one of the biggest differentiators of great managers—the ability to motivate and inspire. We called attention to the importance of managing up and managing laterally, and effective strategies for doing both. We discussed all aspects of how to boost the talent profile and quality of your team. We took a look at some of the rarely talked about challenges you are likely to face at some point in your career as a manager.

It's easy to see from this vantage point just how expansive and nuanced a task it is to master the art and science of effective management. This is precisely why, when beginning our exploration of these topics together, I told you that the greatest leaders are the ones who commit themselves to a lifelong journey of learning. These are not skills and competencies you master overnight. It takes time and true dedication. And there is no end point. We can all elevate our performance. Even the greatest leaders can improve on their weaknesses and build more powerful strengths.

I wish that when I began my own journey as a manager, somebody had shared more with me about what I might be facing so that I could have embraced helpful practices, avoided unnecessary pitfalls, and climbed up my own learning curve with more speed and grace. But I wasn't fortunate enough to have a good mentor in those days.

As I look back on my younger self, I wish somebody had given me some of the essential advice that came to me over the years through my own trials and errors and via the wonderful coaches and mentors who did enter my life further along in my journey.

If I were to give some of that advice to my younger self now, it would be this:

Listen more. Everyone has something to teach you. Seek out advice and mentorship from unexpected places. Absorb as much information and learning as you can early in your professional life because it will pay dividends in the future. Give people your trust. Share the credit generously. Show people you value them early and often. Back this up with simple actions, whether it's asking people for their opinion, thanking them, or simply telling them that their work truly matters. Surround yourself with the best people you possibly can. Hire someone based on potential more than on their immediate readiness to step into a role. Spend more time getting to know people on a personal level. Take people out for coffee or lunch. Build relationships with them. Many of these will turn into lifelong friendships. When you make a mistake or fail, learn from it and move on; don't beat yourself up too much. When you do something great, learn from it and move on; don't be too proud of yourself as your next mistake is usually right around the corner. Control what you can control and let go of the rest. Remember the adage that it takes years to build a reputation but only minutes to destroy it—focus on being a good person above all else. Don't worry so much about what other people may be thinking about you. Don't be too hard on yourself. Focus on doing and being your best and judge yourself by your own inner compass. And most of all, be authentic, genuine, humble, transparent, and empathetic. People remember you most for who you are, not what you accomplish.

I sincerely appreciate how much time and attention you've given to this topic, and to your dedication to becoming the best manager you can be. It truly is a noble profession that provides you with a tremendous opportunity to have a positive impact on people's lives. The world needs more people like you. I wish you nothing but the best in your journey to greatness.